D1526618

DATE DUE

Japanese Military Strategy in the Pacific War

Japanese Military Strategy in the Pacific War

Was Defeat Inevitable?

James B. Wood

ROWMAN & LITTLEFIELD PUBLISHERS, INC.
Lanham • Boulder • New York • Toronto • Plymouth, UK

ROWMAN & LITTLEFIELD PUBLISHERS, INC.

Published in the United States of America
by Rowman & Littlefield Publishers, Inc.
A wholly owned subsidiary of The Rowman & Littlefield Publishing Group, Inc.
4501 Forbes Boulevard, Suite 200, Lanham, Maryland 20706
www.rowmanlittlefield.com

Estover Road, Plymouth PL6 7PY, United Kingdom

Copyright © 2007 by Rowman & Littlefield Publishers, Inc.

British Library Cataloguing in Publication Information Available

Library of Congress Cataloging-in-Publication Data
Wood, James B., 1946-
 Japanese military strategy in the Pacific War : was defeat inevitable? / James B.
Wood.
  p. cm.
 Includes bibliographical references and index.
 ISBN-13: 978-0-7425-5339-2 (cloth : alk. paper)
 ISBN-10: 0-7425-5339-6 (cloth : alk. paper)
 ISBN-13: 978-0-7425-5340-8 (pbk. : alk. paper)
 ISBN-10: 0-7425-5340-X (pbk. : alk. paper)
 1. World War, 1939-1945—Japan. 2. Strategy—History—20th century. 3.
Japan—Military policy. 4. World War, 1939-1945—Pacific Ocean. I. Title.
 D767.2.W66 2007
 940.54'0952—dc22

                                                        2007006497

Printed in the United States of America

♾™ The paper used in this publication meets the minimum requirements of
American National Standard for Information Sciences—Permanence of Paper
for Printed Library Materials, ANSI/NISO Z39.48-1992.

To Daniel

Contents

Preface

Sources on the Pacific War are as vast as the theater itself, and I make no claim to have consulted all or nearly all of them. Nor is this book a scholarly monograph based on decades of original research in the archives. It is an extended, analytical, counterfactual essay on Japanese strategy in World War II—what was and what might have been, based on extensive reading in published documents, official histories, and secondary literature, and for Japanese language sources the translations of others. It is based on my conviction that enough time has passed since 1945—and enough good scholarship produced—to fashion a convincing revisionist argument that Japan's Pacific War defeat by the Allies was not necessarily as inevitable as postwar histories often assume.

One might ask, nevertheless, how a scholar of sixteenth-century France found his way under the big tent of World War II studies. The short answer is that since my undergraduate years, I have been fascinated by military history. I can even faintly recall giving a formal lecture on the battle of the Philippine Sea (the so-called Mariana Turkey Shoot) to an auditorium full of classmates. A second reason is the astonishing intellectual freedom I have had at Williams College to explore and teach on topics other than my necessarily narrow graduate school training. Over the years I gradually began teaching more and more military history (I now offer five different courses in military history including three tutorials) and finally contributed *The King's Army*, a study of the royal French army during the sixteenth-century Wars of Religion, to the ongoing historical debate on the military revolution of Early Modern Europe.

But for the actual genesis of this book, I owe a debt of gratitude to more than a decade of Williams College students who took my tutorial on the

Second World War. There we explored many of the issues and problems inherent to understanding and explaining the course, outcome, and meaning of the war. After listening to several hundred essays and taking part in the discussions that followed, I gradually came to the realization (which I had not had originally) that the totality of Japanese defeat, accepted as inevitable due to American might, obscured what appeared to me to be, at least in its early stages, to borrow from the Duke of Wellington, "a close run thing." For as mighty as Allied forces became, there were real limits to their application in the Pacific theater, where operations were for a long time run on a shoestring. By my reading, the Japanese were not doomed to ultimate military disaster even before the shooting started. Indeed Japanese mistakes and missed opportunities tended to magnify the military advantages of the Allies. Alternate choices existed that, though recognized, were adopted too late or not at all. Japan had the capacity to fight a more successful war, one that could have changed its course in many ways. The reader, of course, will be the judge of just how convincing my case is.

Besides my Williams students, I owe thanks to many for assistance along the way. Williams College provided precious time and funding. Donna Chenail and Peggy Weyers did a superb job of completing the finished draft of the manuscript. My colleagues Robert Dalzell and Thomas Kohut closely read drafts of the manuscript and expressed their enthusiasm for its contents at times when my own flagged. Many of my departmental colleagues attended two History Faculty Colloquia and gave very useful critiques of my earliest ideas on the project. Colleagues Peter Frost and Eiko Maruko, both Japan scholars, read and commented on parts of the manuscript and gave advice on the mysteries of Japanese publishing houses. As for colleagues outside Williams, I owe a special thanks to Professor Steven Ross of the Naval War College for his indefatigable interest and enthusiasm for the project, his historical expertise, and helpful suggestions about possible publishers. Professor Donald Showalter of Colorado College, on little notice, gave a very helpful reading of the entire draft manuscript.

Thanks also to members of my family. My father Brian Wood and brother-in-law Allan Riggs expressed constant curiosity about the project and about when, exactly, it would be finished. My wife Margaret was heavily and helpfully involved in the production of the manuscript at every step along the way. As always I depended upon her love and understanding. My son Daniel read and intelligently critiqued each chapter. To Daniel, but not for that reason, I dedicate the book.

Introduction

Pacific War Redux

Could Japan have won the war? This is a question that has not often been asked by historians. Those who are curious about the Pacific War are much more likely to encounter conclusions put in the guise of questions like "Why were the Japanese so crazy as to take on the United States?" or "How could a country with a GNP about that of Italy, or Canada, expect to win?" or "Why should we expect anything else from a country with a feudal warrior code and culture, emperor worship, racial supremacy notions, and a total lack of sympathy or respect for her neighbors?" The implication is that those responsible for Japan's path to war were ignorant or irrational, perhaps a blend of both, as well as basically evil—a perfectly other counterpoise to the victor of modernity in all respects, the United States.

Recent treatments of the Pacific War are rather straightforward in their explanation of why Japan lost. Ronald Spector's *Eagle Against Sun: The American War With Japan* (1985), an excellent history, concludes:

> So the United States had done the impossible. It had waged war simultaneously on two fronts, separated by thousands of miles, and had prevailed. There had been able leaders and superior strategists on both sides, as well as dedication, bravery, and perseverance. Yet in the end, it was superior American industrial power and organizational ability which had succeeded—as Admiral Yamamoto had foreseen. In the Battle of the Philippine Sea, for example, Japan's strategy had been largely successful. But the Japanese had suffered a devastating defeat because of the superior training, experience, equipment, and numbers of the Americans.[1]

1

Spector at least gives some credit to the Japanese fighting forces, even as he concludes that innate American characteristics and advantages swept over the Japanese empire like a great tidal wave.

Other historians stress a rather basic economic determinism. Military historian John Ellis, in *Brute Force: Allied Strategy and Tactics in the Second World War* (1990), a work dedicated to reducing the Allied war effort to an unskillful, blundering triumph based on sheer material superiority, contends:

> In the last analysis, however, it seems clear that Japanese economic weakness was more than just a matter of their feeble merchant fleet. In fact, even if their supply of raw materials had been absolutely secure for whatever length of time they might have been at war with the United States, they still could not have hoped even remotely to match the massive industrial output of the enemy. Once it became clear that the Americans were not to be bounced out of the ring or psychologically cowed at the first enemy onrush, the Pacific War became a no-contest.[2]

For Ellis, then, Japanese defeat was inevitable under any foreseeable set of events. That position would seem to suggest that the way the war was actually fought in the Pacific was not of much interest or importance.

Of all the books written during the recent fiftieth anniversary of World War II, only one has clearly taken on such deterministic explanations of the course of the war. In *Why the Allies Won* (1995) Richard Overy writes:

> Why did the Allies win World War II? This is such a straightforward question that we assume it has an obvious answer. Indeed the question itself is hardly ever asked. Allied victory is taken for granted. Was their cause not manifestly just? Despite all the dangers, was the progress of their vast forces not irresistible? Explanations of Allied success contain a strong element of determinism. We now know the story so well that we do not consider the uncomfortable prospect that other outcomes might have been possible. To ask why the Allies won is to presuppose that they might have lost or, for understandable reasons, that they would have accepted an outcome short of total victory. These were in fact strong possibilities. There was nothing preordained about Allied success.[3]

In that spirit, this book goes beyond what Japan did to what she could have done, but did not. It explores the vistas that alternative historical roads might have led to if the Japanese had fought a different war, but one that was still within their reach. It is therefore a study both of Japanese defeat and of what was needed to achieve a potential Japanese victory, or at the very least, avoid total ruin. Could Japan have won the war? Obviously not if her military fought the war in the same way as the historical case. But could Japan have fought more effectively? What exactly would that have entailed? What kind of consequences would different actions have had for the course and endgame of the war in the Pacific?

Japan's quest for empire and world power status failed, but it need not have. At the very least, the war's endgame might have been different and more complicated, that is to say more problematic for the Allies than it was. Could Japan have fought a better war? Yes. Could Japan have escaped utter ruin and total defeat? Perhaps. Could the Allies have failed to pursue the war in the Pacific until it was too late to have duplicated their historical triumph? If the war had dragged on for a year or more past its historical end date, what would the postwar world in the Far East look like? Is it possible that the Americans would not have been in a position to demand and for the most part achieve unconditional surrender, the military occupation of Japan, and a total remaking of basic Japanese institutions? All these questions are worth asking. But answers to them, in every case, depend on how the war was fought and when and what both sides were able to achieve militarily.

What then does this book contribute? It is first of all a causal analysis of the events, actions, trends, and decisions that collectively determined when and how the Pacific War was fought and what its outcome was. Unlike much recent work, it does not focus on the personal experiences—the human interest stories, if you will—of those whom the war touched. Other historians and writers have produced sufficient riches in that area.

Second, while it has one shoe firmly planted in the familiar territory of military studies and history, the other is firmly placed in the camp of counterfactual studies. The book tries to think through the alternative historical possibilities that existed during the Pacific War—what might have happened if important aspects of the war had followed, to borrow the title of Robert Frost's famous verse, "The Road Not Taken."[4] But unlike some counterfactual projects, it is not a faux narrative of a reimagined historical world. It is instead an extended argument that concentrates on the most essential military factors at work in the unfolding of the Pacific War, the parameters within which those factors operated, or could have operated, and what the significance of a different path within those historical parameters might have been. It examines how familiar events could have become more complicated or problematic under different, but nevertheless historically possible conditions.

It is also a system-wide analysis, one that posits that somewhat different outcomes could have resulted from the impact of cumulative changes in the way the war was fought by Japan rather than singular incidents and personalities. A number of "What If?" books explore alternative historical outcomes for various aspects of World War II.[5] For the most part they focus on dramatic individual events. For example, what if at Midway American dive bombers had not attacked the Japanese carriers refueling and rearming their planes on flight decks during a brief twenty to thirty minute window of opportunity, sinking them all? Or, what if Douglas MacArthur had perished during his flight from the Philippines in 1942? The alternatives analyzed in this account do not depend on such signal individual historical events or dramatic accidents. They rest instead on changes in the complicated interaction of many different kinds of operational factors over fairly long stretches of time.

Readers will also not find here any treatment of such things as war crimes, mistreatment of prisoners, perverse biochemical and medical experiments, mutilation of the dead, propaganda, the primacy of cultural attitudes, the nature of collective public memories of the war, or doubts about the motives and reasons for the dropping of the atomic bombs. Many historians believe such phenomena to be the most important aspects of the war, often at the expense of the war itself as a subject. John Dower, for example, in *War Without Mercy*, argues that:

> To understand how racism influenced the conduct of the war in Asia has required going beyond the formal documents and battle reports upon which historians normally rely and drawing on materials such as songs, movies, cartoons, and a wide variety of popular as well as academic writings published at the time. . . . The greatest challenge has not been to recall the raw emotions of the war, however, but rather to identify dynamic patterns in the torrent of war words and graphic images—and to bring such abstractions to earth by demonstrating how stereotyped and often blatantly racist thinking contributed to poor military intelligence and planning, atrocious behavior, and the adoption of exterminationist policies.[6]

Racial attitudes, in his view, trumped military science. The main problem with such an approach is that it decenters the fundamental military exigencies that underlie modern warfare and replaces them with epiphenomena, though recent books like Richard Frank's *Downfall: The End of the Imperial Japanese Empire* and Allison Gilmore's *You Can't Fight Tanks With Bayonets* have gone a long way toward discrediting many of the assumptions and much of the evidence such work depends on.[7] This book, on the other hand, is very much a study of the exigencies and instrumentalities of the Pacific War, not public attitudes and cultural stereotypes.

To that end the first chapter explores Japan's path to war, finding it opportunistic but not irrational. The second chapter then examines what went wrong—why Japan's early war successes were followed by an unbroken string of defeats. The third then pinpoints what would have had to change in Japan's system of waging war if she was to avoid her historical fate. The remaining five chapters each concentrate on one of the most important instruments of Japanese war making—the merchant marine, the submarine force, the battle fleet, army and navy air forces, and the imperial army's ground forces—and explain the ways in which a different and more successful war could have been waged against the Allies in each of these areas. The conclusion combines the results of these inquiries and posits that fighting a different war was well within the historical capacities of imperial Japan. The Japanese had good opportunities, even if they did not capitalize on them, to modify the course of the war in their favor. If those alternative roads had been traveled, the end of the Pacific War and the shape of the postwar era would have differed significantly from the historical counterparts with which we are all so familiar and, perhaps a little too complacently, accept as in the natural run of things. My insistence that the Japanese had the potential to mount a much more effective military resistance, however, is not in any way intended to diminish the Allied effort in the Pacific. It rather underscores the fact that the enormous task of achieving total military victory over Japan would have been even more difficult, perhaps too difficult, if the Japanese had fought a different war and the Allies had not actually fought the war as skillfully as they did. The history of the war in the Pacific was not written in stone from its beginning.

NOTES

1. Ronald H. Spector, *Eagle Against Sun: The American War with Japan* (New York: Vintage Books, 1985), 560.
2. John Ellis, *Brute Force. Allied Strategy and Tactics in the Second World War* (New York: Viking, 1990), 477.
3. Richard Overy, *Why the Allies Won* (New York: Norton, 1995), 1.
4. Edward Connery Lathem, ed., *The Poetry of Robert Frost* (New York: Holt, Rinehart and Winston, 1969), 105.
5. See, for example, Robert Cowley and Steven E. Ambrose, eds., *What If? The World's Foremost Military Historians Imagine What Might Have Been* (New York: Putnam, 1998); Harold C. Deutsch and Dennis E. Showalter, eds., *What If? Strategic Alternatives of World War II* (USA: Emperor's Press, 1997); Peter G. Tsouras, ed., *Rising Sun Victorious: The Alternate History of How the Japanese Won the Pacific War* (Mechanicsburg, PA: Stackpole Books, 2001).
6. John W. Dower, *War Without Mercy. Race and Power in the Pacific War* (New York: Pantheon, 1986), x.
7. Richard B. Frank, *Downfall: The End of the Imperial Japanese Empire* (New York: Random House, 1999); Allison B. Gilmore, *You Can't Fight Tanks with Bayonets: Psychological Warfare Against the Japanese Army in the Southwest Pacific* (Lincoln: University of Nebraska Press, 1998).

1

Going to War

The great irony of the Pacific War is that the virtually flawless execution of Japan's initial strategic plans resulted within less than a year not in victory but in a series of significant defeats that left the strategic initiative in the hands of the enemy. This outcome is often used as proof that Japan's decision to go to war with the Western powers in late 1941 was an enormous mistake. This book will argue, to the contrary, that the war against the Allies was the right war at the right time for Japan. By the end of the 1930s her international intransigence and naked military aggression had created a situation in which the survival of Japan as a great power, and of her conception of an Asian empire, did indeed hang in the balance. By the fall of 1941 the question had come to be not whether there was to be war with the Western powers, including the latently powerful United States, but, given the regional and world situation, whether there would ever come a more favorable time to solve Japan's resource problems by military action. As her overwhelming early victories should remind us, the decision to go to war was based on a correct calculation of the balance of power in Asia and the military risks involved. It was only when a sound original strategic plan to secure the resources Japan needed and to establish a defensible perimeter for the empire and its new conquests was superseded by needless overexpansion that the enemy was able to regain the initiative and lock Japanese forces into a premature war of attrition they had not intended nor were prepared to fight.[1] This was, however, an avoidable outcome, and the Pacific War could easily have turned out differently.

Many military histories depict the Japanese decision to go to war as an almost irrational or even suicidal national act. Contempt toward the West and miscalculation of the impact of naked aggression on American opinion, according to this view, blinded Japanese leaders to America's tremendous military potential and its ability ultimately to crush Japan materially. Certainly such willful ignorance played a role in some circles, but even within the military there were many influential officers who had a fairly clear idea and accurate intelligence about America's actual and potential military power.[2] It should also be remembered that Japan's decision to go to war against the Western powers was taken after long and careful deliberation—it was not a spur of the moment action. Though the decision was influenced by both fear and opportunism, it represented above all a *calculated* risk.

That some Japanese leaders urged caution or argued against war is also sometimes used to underline the supposed irresponsibility of the pro-war factions in pushing for war. It is true that many prominent individuals recorded feelings of dread and foreboding on the eve of war, but similar thoughts were expressed by leaders in every combatant country on the eve of World War II. Too much concentration on the divisions and hesitations among the ruling elite obscures the fact that in Japan in 1941, everyone—civilian or military—who held responsible positions of power, even so-called moderates, were ardent nationalists and staunch supporters of the imperial vision. With the exception of a few extremists, they shared a common intellectual formation and worldview that, as a recent study reminds us, was essentially identical to that of the emperor himself.[3] A better question to ask might be why, in the fall of 1941, they all believed that Japan's very national existence was threatened.

The seizure of Manchuria in 1931 and subsequent organization of Manchuko had been wildly popular in Japan.[4] But war in China proper from 1937 on had become an increasingly expensive and intractable commitment. Japan controlled much of China and had driven Nationalist forces far into the interior, but she could not bring the Chinese government to surrender or negotiate. Then, in 1940, settlement of the China Incident became directly linked to events in Europe. Germany's defeat of France and the Netherlands left tiny white imperialist regimes in the resource-rich territories of Southeast Asia isolated and vulnerable. In order to block one of the last supply routes into China, Japan in July 1940 forced Vichy France to agree to Japanese occupation of northern Vietnam, while Great Britain, fighting for its survival at home, temporarily acquiesced to Japanese pressure by closing the Burma Road.

International opinion had been outraged by brutalities committed by Japanese forces in China.[5] The move into Vietnam, followed in November by the signing of the Tripartite Pact with Nazi Germany and fascist Italy, hardened American attitudes. Besides continuing public recognition of the nationalist regime and financial credits to bolster Chinese resistance, the

American response to Japanese aggression in Manchuria and China was to enact trade embargoes on strategic materials, particularly oil and metals that were essential to the continued operation of the Japanese economy as well as its military machine. The Japanese occupation of southern Vietnam in July 1941 proved to be the last straw for the United States. In August President Roosevelt froze all Japanese assets in the United States and cut off export of high-grade octane to Japan. Similar actions by the British and Dutch soon followed. Suddenly Japan's access to vital resources was restricted to the empire itself and occupied territory. The embargo on oil and gasoline products, in particular, alarmed Imperial General Headquarters (IGHQ), which estimated that Japan's petroleum reserves on hand could last for only another two years and then would be totally exhausted, with no source of replenishment in sight.[6]

But the threat to Japan was not purely economic. Strategic moves by the United States, such as the adoption of a massive navy building program, the movement of the Pacific Fleet from San Diego to Pearl Harbor, secret military talks with the so-called ABCD group (America-Britain-China-Netherlands), and the belated but significant buildup of U.S. ground and air forces in the Philippines (as well as Commonwealth forces in Malaya) also greatly alarmed the military. The threat to Japan's continued national existence as a great power and her preeminence in Asia could not have been clearer.

The final decision for war, then, rested on a realistic appraisal of the international situation, national and imperial interests, and Japan's level of military preparedness. American hostility to Japan's position in Asia was manifest and in retrospect, the conclusion that the United States was bent on war was in no way a misreading of American intentions. Japan's access to resources outside the empire proper was cut off and reserves were quite limited. Continuing peace with the ABCD countries could obviously not redress that situation while military action would provide Japan with the resources needed to fight the kind of protracted industrial war that the Allies would be sure to favor. The balance of military power in the region immediately favored Japan because potential enemy forces were understrength, generally of poor quality, scattered over vast distances, and isolated within a sea of indifferent or even hostile indigenous subjects. It was also clear by the fall of 1941 that too much delay would allow the United States in particular to improve its Asian and Pacific defenses significantly and provide vital time for its overall military mobilization. The Russian threat to the north, which had manifested itself in a severe beating administered to Kwantung Army forces in western Manchuria in 1939, was for the short term neutralized by the signing of a nonaggression pact with the Soviet Union, and perhaps even for the long term if German victories on the Eastern Front continued. And defeat of Western forces and their ejection from East Asia might finally provide the leverage to bring the Chinese to their senses.[7]

It would be difficult indeed to imagine a more potent mixture of very real threats to Japan's imperial survival and an emerging international situation that provided a fleeting opportunity, perhaps soon to be reversed, to take military advantage of weak, scattered, and unprepared enemy forces. The fact was that Japan found herself in a situation in which even the most moderate elements, including Hirohito himself, were forced to conclude that national survival was at stake.

Since World War I, and especially during the 1930s when Japan began her enormous military buildup, the army and navy had ruthlessly competed with each other for funding, the former obsessively oriented toward Manchuria and China, the latter the western Pacific, the mandated islands, and the coming decisive battle with the American fleet. Despite the fact that the services went their own separate ways, as the scope and scale of military preparation and involvement increased, it became obvious that some over-all coordination of military resources and planning was necessary. To meet this need, Imperial General Headquarters was created in 1937, at the beginning of the China war. IGHQ included the ministry heads and Chiefs of General Staff of both services, and it was there that the rival services hammered out written agreements specifying their respective roles and responsibilities in planning and interservice coordination. Larger issues of national policy were discussed and decided at IGHQ-Government Liaison Conferences attended by the prime minister and Cabinet officials in addition to IGHQ. Final and formal approval of national policy took place at Imperial Conferences presided over by the emperor. The most singular aspect of these arrangements, of course, was the lack of civilian control over the armed forces, for the service heads retained complete autonomy in military matters and were accountable only to the emperor, to whom they had direct access. It was in these institutional settings that, as pressure to bring the China war to a successful conclusion mounted and as Japan's international isolation grew, appraisal of the military and world situation was done and decisions about war and peace were made.[8]

The first formal steps toward war took place at the Imperial Conference of July 2, 1941, where it was resolved that Japan should not avoid war with the United States and Great Britain in pursuing her southern policies. On September 6, in light of the still unimproved diplomatic situation, another Imperial Conference ordered preparations for war to be rushed to completion by the end of October. Though negotiations would continue, they would proceed in parallel with planning for war with the West. However, after the Hull Memo of October 2—which was effectively an ultimatum to withdraw from China—any diplomatic settlement to the developing crisis seemed doomed, and at another Imperial Conference on November 5, a decision was made to go to war if no diplomatic solution had been reached by early December. The government, with at least the formal approval of the army and navy, continued contacts with the Americans, but it was clear that the Japanese and American positions on the evacuation of Vietnam and ending the China war were irreconcilable. In the meantime, the Army-Navy Central Agreement was signed in Tokyo on November 10, followed by detailed operational orders in mid-November. The final decision to launch Japan into war was made on November 29 and confirmed at an Imperial Conference on December 1, and the next day the actual attack date was fixed for December 8. The emperor, who bore a silent but major share of responsibility for Japanese actions in China, was heavily involved in both the planning of the previous months and the decision to go to war.[9]

The possibility of war with the United States, of course, was hardly a new concept for Japanese leaders. Since early in the century, America and Russia respectively had been identified as the major strategic threats to Japanese hegemony in the western Pacific and on the Asian mainland. Japanese Army and Navy planning and force structures had been tailored to meet these respective threats. From the point of view of the Pacific, in fact, Japanese and American war plans were eerie reverse images of each other. In case of war with Japan, the Americans intended a naval advance across the central Pacific followed by a decisive defeat of the Japanese battle fleet and subsequent blockade and bombardment of the home islands. There the Japanese Navy planned to await the American Fleet where, reduced by attrition and at the end of an untenable supply line, it would be destroyed in a Mahanian-type decisive battle reminiscent of Tsushima in 1905.[10]

Even before the fall 1941 decisions to go to war, military staffs and agencies had begun preparing and critiquing plans, initiating special training programs, and positioning military assets and units. But in its final form, the war plan departed in two crucial ways from the traditional plan of inflicting sharp defeats on Allied military forces in Malaya and the Philippines while waiting for the decisive fleet action with the Pacific Fleet in the western Pacific. The first significant departure, of course, was that the plan involved expansion, consolidation, and exploitation outside the empire proper on an unprecedented scale. The major purpose of operations was the rapid seizure of whole resource rich regions and their populations to the south followed by the establishment of a defensive perimeter running along the Burma-Malaya-Dutch East Indies-Northwest New Guinea-Mandates-Home Islands-Kuriles line.

The amphibious nature of the proposed operations required close cooperation between the army and the navy and the temporary requisitioning of about half of Japan's merchant fleet tonnage for military purposes. Gaining and maintaining air superiority with a combination of land and carrier-based planes was also essential to the plan. To mount these operations, the army had to temporarily shelve its plans for war with the Soviet Union but because of commitments in Manchuria and China, was only willing to provide eleven divisions and about half its air strength, along with supporting units, to the southern operation. So from the early stages of planning basically the entire strength of the navy and its air units had to be committed to taking part in the southward advance as well as maintaining preparedness to ward off any westward movement of the U.S. Fleet in the decisive battle.[11]

It was here that the second crucial departure from traditional planning occurred. As early as January 1941, Admiral Yamamoto, commander in chief of Combined Fleet, had begun to entertain thoughts of a preemptive carrier strike against the U.S. Fleet at Pearl Harbor, a notion that departed entirely from both the traditional and current navy planning. Delivering a crippling blow to American battleships and carriers at Pearl Harbor would, of course, eliminate any immediate threat to the eastward flank of the Japanese advance and guarantee the time needed to take and organize the newly conquered areas. But the disadvantages of such an operation were obvious: the diversion of naval strength needed for the amphibious main thrust south and the needless risk of major fleet carrier units which, if lost, would significantly weaken imperial defenses at the very start of the war. Though the attack on Pearl Harbor was fiercely opposed by the Navy General Staff (NGS), Yamamoto prevailed in the end by threatening to resign as commander of the Combined Fleet on the very eve of operations.[12]

In its final form the Japanese plan was breathtaking in its scope and ambition. What years before had begun as a fairly simple plan to defend imperial waters and territory, in other words, had crystallized in an era of international turmoil into a plan to destroy the U.S. Fleet in its home waters, seize control of the Western colonial empires in the East, and establish military domination over the entire western and central Pacific. Given the relatively limited forces and tremendous distances involved, success would depend upon surprise, speed, concentration of force, and the ability to reuse the forces involved in the initial operations in the later stages of the advance. Proof that the calculations of risks on which the proposed operations were based were correct and that the right moment to strike had been chosen, lay, of course, in the achievements of the Japanese military in the first months of war.

On December 8, America's Pacific Fleet at Pearl Harbor was dealt a severe, though not fatal, blow. From forward staging areas in China, Formosa, and Vietnam, Japanese naval, air, and ground forces rapidly moved south at astonishing speed. Malaya and the Philippines were invaded on the first day of operations. Hong Kong fell on December 25, Manila on January 2. By January 12, Japanese forces were landing in the Dutch East Indies. Forces from the Mandates reached Rabaul on January 23. Singapore, the bastion of the British Far East, surrendered on February 15; formal resistance in the Dutch East Indies ended on March 9. By late March, Japanese forces had

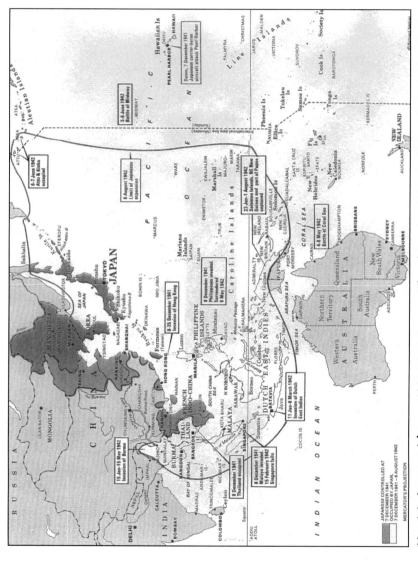

Map 1.1. Japanese Advance, 1941–1942. *Source: Atlas of American Wars*, by Richard Natkiel. Bison Books, 1986.

seized all the essential objectives needed to establish a new and expanded National Defense Zone. Losses had been minimal. Only in the Philippines, where American and Filipino forces held out until early May, did fighting continue. The Allies found themselves temporarily capable of only small-scale harassing tactics on the periphery of the newly conquered areas and were thought unlikely by IGHQ to be able to mount a strong counteroffensive before mid-1943.[13]

Defeat of the Allies proceeded so swiftly and easily that debate about what the next stage of operations should entail had already begun by January 1942. But there was little unanimity within IGHQ or even the individual services as to what the next steps should be. At its heart, the debate revolved around the question of whether Japanese forces should be rested and refitted while her military position was consolidated and strengthened, or whether taking advantage of the temporary absence of significant Allied opposition, they should push on beyond the original planned limits. In the short run, Japan retained the initiative, and the sudden collapse of Allied opposition in the East made arguments for expanded operations attractive. On the other hand, the rapid success of operations had left Japan without a fully worked out overall strategic plan for developing an effective National Defense Zone to thwart future Allied attacks. There was great pressure to return requisitioned merchant shipping to civilian usage according to the original timetable, and the army and navy were now operating at the end of an immensely long line of communications that would be stretched even further by continued expansion.

Since the Japanese Army saw the Pacific War primarily as an extension of the China war, it wanted to turn its attention back to the mainland once the initial stage of the southern advance had been successfully concluded. It preferred to leave minimum garrison forces in the southern area and limit its support for any further outward operations. There was, therefore, strong army opposition to any expansion beyond the areas that had already been secured, particularly if it called for the substantial commitment of its forces. The navy, oriented to the oceanic areas and less tied to static concepts of defense than the army, strongly pushed for operations beyond the original limits in order to deny to the enemy as many forward bases as possible. An initial idea for an invasion of the Hawaiian Islands, and subsequently an invasion of northern Australia, were vetoed by the army on the grounds that it could not provide sufficient forces nor, given shipping constraints, possibly support them at those distances.[14]

Agreement on second stage operations was nevertheless finally achieved at an IGHQ Government Liaison Conference in early March 1942. There both services adopted a strategy of strengthening Japan's position by capturing key points beyond the areas that had been occupied during the first stage of operations, including the Aleutians, Port Moresby on the southern

New Guinea coast, New Caledonia, Fiji, and Samoa in the South Pacific. The army, satisfied because it expected that it would not have to provide many troops for these operations, ordered the return of five divisions to the mainland for the final reckoning with the Chinese. The navy also got what it wanted: an aggressive expansion on the periphery. This decision to continue what were referred to as "Outer Perimeter" operations was a major strategic blunder, for it was on that perimeter that mistakes would be made that would lead later to the rapid and total defeat of Japan.[15]

Seizure of forward outposts was not, in and of itself, bad strategy. Port Moresby, for example, could provide a valuable early warning system for the developing center for southern operations at Rabaul, in the Admiralty Islands, while the southeast Pacific islands were well suited as a springboard for long-range reconnaissance and attacks on the U.S. supply line to Australia. A fundamental problem, however, was that while such places might be taken, they could not be logistically supported on any reasonable basis. Maintaining a base on Fiji, for example, meant a three thousand mile round-trip beyond Rabaul. At least as important, once taken, such places could not be held if attacked by numerically superior Allied forces. And the enemy would always be in a position to concentrate major forces at any single point on the perimeter.

Most critically, Japanese expansion beyond the limits of the original national defense zone was a needless provocation that, for both political and military reasons, would force a desperate and rapid American response. IGHQ had calculated that in a war against both Japan and Germany the United States probably would concentrate on Europe, giving Japan enough time to eliminate British and Dutch resistance in the Far East before the United States could move in force into the Pacific. This assumption was correct, for prewar American plans, especially after the fall of France in 1940, did intend in the case of war with both Germany and Japan to remain on the defensive in the Pacific and to concentrate on victory in Europe, and this so-called "Germany First" plan was quickly reaffirmed by Roosevelt and Churchill after Pearl Harbor. By moving beyond the core of the newly conquered resource areas and directly threatening Australia and its line of communications with the United States, Japan convinced even adamant supporters of the "Germany First" strategy, like Generals Marshall and Arnold, to agree with great reluctance that the situation was grave enough to justify a rapid buildup of defensive forces in the south and southwest Pacific. The threat of continued Japanese expansion, in other words, checkmated American plans to stand strictly on the defensive in the Pacific. A Japanese decision to hold to the originally planned limits of the advance, on the other hand, would have allowed the United States to do almost nothing in the Pacific while she turned her energies to the Battle of the Atlantic and a quick invasion of the European continent. In fact, it is interesting to speculate on the possible impact of a public pronouncement by Japanese officials that the empire had already reached its limits and that no further goals in the New Guinea-Australia-South Pacific area would be pursued. This would have presented a clear problem to those American planners, like Admiral King, who favored a quicker and stronger response in the Pacific.

In this same context, the Combined Fleet was itself about to depart from its traditional defensive posture in the central Pacific. Following Pearl Harbor, the fleet continued to support the other first-stage operations but always held powerful forces in readiness or subject to immediate recall to form a striking force against any remnants of the American fleet advancing from Hawaii. Despite the preponderance of battleship officers in the upper ranks, Pearl Harbor and the advance south had dramatically confirmed the importance of carrier and land-based airpower in the huge spaces and island environment of the Pacific. As the Allies had learned to their regret, defending this vast area would be difficult. To prevent the American carrier and amphibious forces from simply turning the tide by attacking isolated bases required an extensive system of interlocking land-based naval airpower combined with a mobile striking force: a modern Mahanian fleet-in-being with carrier forces that could rapidly respond to any attempt to pierce the defensive perimeter. To prepare for this role, the prudent course in the spring of 1942, and the course favored by the Navy General Staff, was to rest and refit the fleet, especially the carrier forces which had been in continuous operation since Pearl Harbor.

Once again, however, Admiral Yamamoto began to push his own particular brand of overextension. He knew that the American carriers had escaped unscathed from the Pearl Harbor attack. This left the Pacific Fleet with a still formidable offensive punch that soon manifested itself in successful carrier task force raids against Japanese outposts in the southwest and central Pacific. How to eliminate this threat exercised Yamamoto, who had grown increasingly impatient with the traditional strategy of waiting for a showdown with the enemy fleet in the western Pacific. His concerns were intensified by the mid-April Doolittle raid on Tokyo, and he and key members of his staff concluded that the best way to end the threat of carrier raids was to seize the initiative by attacking and occupying Midway Island, the westernmost of the Hawaiian chain. A clear and dire threat to Midway, they thought, would lure the American carriers out of Pearl Harbor to be crushed in a decisive fleet action, finally eliminating the Pacific Fleet as a serious threat.[16]

The Navy General Staff strongly resisted Yamamoto's plan. Midway was not much of a strategic prize. Over two thousand miles east of the fleet anchorages in the Home Islands, even if captured, it could not be maintained logistically without a massive diversion of scarce merchant shipping, just like the new objectives to the south. Since the Combined Fleet could not operate there indefinitely and the size of the island drastically limited the size of any garrison, American forces staging from Hawaii could easily retake the base anytime they wanted. Finally, and perhaps most critically, it seemed to the NGS utterly reckless to risk major fleet elements, particularly the bulk of the carrier arm, so far from any area that was vital to the empire and beyond the range of supporting land-based aircraft. Yamamoto and his staff had no effective arguments to counter these objections, but the admiral's personal prestige was so unassailable after Pearl Harbor that another explicit threat to resign as commander in chief of the Combined Fleet forced the ultimate acceptance of the operation.[17]

As finally developed, the attack on Midway involved massive forces that created major security and coordination problems, as well as the diversion of valuable fleet assets northwards to the Aleutians. Furthermore, carrier losses earlier at the battle of the Coral Sea made it impossible for the First Air Fleet to provide enough carrier-based planes to guarantee a decisive numerical advantage over the defenders. Though American intelligence at first dismissed evidence of a central Pacific advance against Midway on the grounds that such an attack lacked any clear military rationale, in the end the code breakers and radio traffic analysts were able to predict accurately the scale and timing of the attack, enabling Nimitz to assemble enough Midway and carrier-based aircraft to match Japanese numbers.[18] Then chance, even pure dumb luck, helped the Americans send all four of the Japanese fleet carriers in the covering force to the bottom. In a matter of hours, half of the Japanese carrier arm's capacity was lost. Though the Americans also sustained heavy losses, they were in no way as critical to their general military posture in the central Pacific as were those of the Japanese.

Midway is often characterized as the decisive defeat that cost Japan the war as well as a battle that should have never been fought. It substantially negated much of Japan's early strategic advantages and would have negative repercussions on her entire military position, for the lost Japanese carrier forces were to have been the key component of the fleet-in-being rapid response force needed to contest, in combination with land-based aircraft, future American advances. It was also a perfect example of the so-called "Victory Disease" mentality that had taken hold among the more reckless officers in the navy. As damaging as it was, however, the fact remained that the U.S. Navy did not yet have sufficient strength to launch a powerful counteroffensive through the central Pacific. The main question was the same after Midway as before: how was Japan going to consolidate its holdings, lay the groundwork for an extended war, and prepare the national defense zone for the inevitable return of the Allies?

Even though the navy initially withheld accurate information about the true nature of the losses at Midway from the army, the missing carriers soon caused the cancellation of the New Caledonia-Fiji-Samoa operations. Other

Outer Perimeter operations nevertheless went forward. An initial attempt to take Port Moresby by sea had been turned back in May, but soon after Midway there was a renewed attempt to take Port Moresby by attacking across the Owen Stanley Mountains, thereby threatening Australia. More than five hundred miles southeast of Rabaul, in the Solomon Islands, construction was begun on an airfield on Guadalcanal near the seaplane base on neighboring Tulagi, from which Japanese naval air units could monitor Allied naval operations to the south and east and menace the shipping lanes from the U.S. west coast to New Zealand and Australia.

These aggressive moves triggered an immediate enemy response that caught IGHQ by surprise. Realizing that the results of Midway gave them increased strategic flexibility, the U.S. Joint Chiefs increased the flow of American troops and planes to the Pacific and went over to the offensive in the South Pacific. In eastern New Guinea MacArthur's southwest Pacific Area forces fought the overextended and unsupplied Japanese thrust against Port Moresby to a halt, forced it back over the mountains, and began a multipronged advance on Buna on the northeast New Guinea coast. In early August American marines landed on Guadalcanal, seizing the almost completed airfield there. For the Japanese high command, the focus of the entire war suddenly shifted from China to the Pacific.[19]

The Japanese riposte to these Allied moves was swift, aggressive, and ultimately disastrous. Egged on by the emperor, the Imperial General Headquarters began pouring reinforcements of naval, air, and ground forces into a desperate attritional struggle for Guadalcanal, a place that, like Midway, was hardly critical to the defense of the empire.[20] At the absolute limit of its air cover, the Japanese forces enjoyed none of their early advantages. Naval and air losses, in particular, climbed to alarming levels. American losses were also heavy, but they were able to replace their losses and keep their forces supplied and slowly build up enough local superiority of numbers that it was simply logistically impossible for Japan to sustain the struggle. In December, IGHQ concluded that withdrawal was the only course left and evacuated the diseased remnants of its forces from the island in February 1943.[21] But the fighting and the losses did not stop there. The Americans slowly began clawing their way up the Solomons toward Rabaul, and Allied forces under MacArthur methodically advanced along the northern New Guinea coast. As Japanese naval, air, and shipping losses continued to be severe, a constant drain of military resources to the struggle on the periphery took place, which left the defenses and support infrastructure of the original national defense zone almost entirely unfinished. By the end of 1943, Japanese naval and air forces were so reduced and the enemy's growing material advantage so large that when the Americans attacked in strength, there was little left to slow or stop their advance.

Recent histories of the Pacific War emphasize how the military results of the period from roughly mid-1942 to mid-1943 were critical in determining, after so promising a beginning, the defeat of Japan.[22] The fact that this dramatic reversal took place even before the balance of power had tipped in favor of the Allies might appear to be evidence that Japan's entry into the war had indeed been a terrible mistake, a kind of teleological unfolding of a predetermined tragedy. The abrupt replacement of victory by defeats in 1942 can be directly traced to decisions to launch the so-called Outer Perimeter operations and to risk the carrier force on another Hawaiian gamble. But it is the contention of this book that this outcome was not inevitable. Not only could the outcome have been different, it was within the power of the Japanese to have made it different. Midway, New Guinea, and Guadalcanal were the wrong battles fought at the wrong places at the wrong times. And there were alternatives. A vigorous pursuit of the original plans for a strongly fortified national defense zone, better coordination of resources, avoidance of attritional battles, as well as other equally obvious measures, many of which were actually considered, could have systematically improved Japan's position. How such errors could have been avoided, what should have been done, and how that could have changed the face of the Pacific War will be explored in the rest of the book.

NOTES

1. The best general history of the war is Gerald L. Weinberg, *A World at War: A Global History of World War II* (New York: Cambridge University Press, 1994). A good atlas with excellent text is David Smurthwaite, *The Pacific War Atlas, 1941–1945* (London: Mirabel Books, 1995). For a chronology and a close look at different locations in the Pacific area, see Gordon L. Rottman, *World War II Pacific Island Guide: A Geo-Military Study* (Westport, CT: Greenwood Press, 2002).

2. John Ellis, *Brute Force* (New York: Viking, 2000), 443–46.

3. See Herbert P. Bix, *Hirohito and the Making of Modern Japan* (New York: Harper Collins, 2000).

4. See the brilliant study by Louise Young, *Japan's Total Empire: Manchuria and the Culture of Wartime Imperialism* (Berkeley: University of California Press, 1998). By far the most comprehensive treatment of the Kwantung Army is Alvin D. Coox, *Nomonhan: Japan Against Russia, 1939* (Palo Alto, CA: Stanford University Press, 1985), 2 vols. Another excellent study of the prewar army is L. A. Humphreys, *The Way of the Heavenly Sword: The Japanese Army in the 1920's* (Palo Alto, CA: Stanford University Press, 1995). For a good general history of the rise and fall of the army, see Meirion Harries and Susie Harries, *Soldiers of the Sun: The Rise and Fall of the Imperial Japanese Army* (New York: Random House, 1991).

5. See Iris Chang, *The Rape of Nanking. The Forgotten Holocaust of World War II* (New York: Basic Books, 1997); Katsuichi Honda, *The Nanking Massacre*, trans.

Karen Sandness, ed. Frank Gibney (Armonk, NY: M. E. Sharpe, 1999); Mashiro Yamamoto, *Nanking: Anatomy of an Atrocity* (Westport, CT: Praeger Publishers, 2000);
and for later atrocities, Yuki Tanaka, *Hidden Horrors: Japanese War Crimes in World
War II* (Boulder, CO: Westview Press, 1996).

    6. General Douglas MacArthur, *The Reports of General MacArthur*, vol. 1, pt. 1,
Japanese Operations in the Southwest Pacific Area (Washington, DC: Department of the
Army, 1966, 1950), 44–58. The second volume of *Reports of MacArthur* is a very rich
source based on postwar interrogations of Japanese officers. There is a good critique
of the decision to go to war and Japanese strategy in Alvin D. Coox, "The Effectiveness of the Japanese Military Establishment in the Second World War," in Allan R.
Millett and Williamson Murray, *Military Effectiveness*, vol. 3, *The Second World War*
(Boston: Allen & Unwin, 1988), 1–44. On the general problem of imports and shipping, and especially of oil, see the excellent study by Mark P. Parillo, *The Japanese
Merchant Marine in World War II* (Annapolis, MD: Naval Institute Press, 1993),
39–62.

    7. Bix, *Hirohito*, 387–487; Edward J. Drea, *In the Service of the Emperor: Essays on
the Imperial Japanese Army* (Lincoln: University of Nebraska Press, 1998), 26–41,
169–215.

    8. Bix, *Hirohito*, 317–85.

    9. Ibid., 387–497.

    10. Spector, *Eagle Against Sun*, 33–71, and Ronald A. Spector, *At War At Sea:
Sailors and Naval Combat in the Twentieth Century* (New York: Viking, 2001), 1–21.
For a close look at prewar U.S. strategy in the Pacific, see Stephen T. Ross, *American
War Plans, 1941–1945. The Test of Battle* (Portland, OR: Frank Cass, 1997); Brian
McAllister Linn, *Guardians of Empire: The U.S. Army and the Pacific, 1902–1940*
(Chapel Hill: University of North Carolina Press, 1997); and Samuel E. Morison,
History of United States Naval Operations in World War II, vol. 3, *The Rising Sun in the
Pacific, 1931–April 1942* (Boston: Little, Brown & Co., 1951), 3–79. Hereafter the se-
ries title will be cited as, *HUSNO*.

    11. Saburo Hayashi, *Kōgun: The Japanese Army in the Pacific War* (Quantico, VA:
The Marine Corps Association; 1959, Reprint 1989), 29–33. Hayashi is particularly
good on army-navy relations. *Reports of General MacArthur*, vol. 2, pt. 2, 62. On the
development of Japanese amphibious capabilities, Drea, *Service of the Emperor*,
13–25.

    12. Spector, *Eagle Against Sun*, 78–82; Morison, vol. 3, *Rising Sun*, 81–87; Paul S.
Dull, *A Battle History of the Imperial Japanese Navy (1941–45)* (Annapolis, MD: Naval
Institute Press, 1978), 3–10.

    13. Indispensable for strategic background, reactions, decisions, and the chain of
events is Louis Morton, *Strategy and Command: The First Two Years* (Washington, DC:
Department of the Army, 1962). See also for this early period the excellent study by
H. P. Willmott, *The War with Japan: The Period of Balance, May 1942–October 1943*
(Wilmington, DE: S. R. Books, 2002). For Japanese strategy, Hayashi, *Kōgun*, passim;
and Dull, *Battle History*, passim.

    14. Spector, *Eagle Against Sun*, 151–55; Willmott, *The War with Japan*, 3–12.

    15. Hayashi, *Kōgun*, 41–47.

    16. Spector, *Eagle Against Sun*, 151–55; Hayashi, *Kōgun*, 51–57; Willmott, *The
War with Japan*, 13–18.

17. On the Midway campaign, John Keegan, *The Price of Admiralty: The Evolution of Naval Warfare* (New York: Viking, 1989), 157–211; Spector, *At War At Sea*, 198–204; Mitsuo Fuchida and Masatake Okumiya, *Midway. The Battle that Doomed Japan, the Japanese Navy's Story*, trans. Masataki Chihaya (Annapolis, MD: Naval Institute Press, 1992 [2001]), passim.

18. John Prados, *Combined Fleet Decoded: The Secret History of American Intelligence and the Japanese Navy in World War II* (New York: Random House, 1995), 195–335. Willmott, *The War with Japan*, 19–35.

19. Bix, *Hirohito*, 449.

20. On the emperor's role see Bix, *Hirohito*, 439–462, esp. 455–460. On his penchant for pursuing decisive victories, see the excellent accounting by Drea in "Chasing a Decisive Victory," in *In the Service of the Emperor*, 168–215. The best treatment of the Guadalcanal campaign in all its aspects and from the perspective of both sides is Richard B. Frank, *Guadalcanal: The Definitive Account of the Landmark Battle* (New York: Random House, 1990). See also Samuel E. Morison, HUSNO, vol. 5, *The Struggle to Guadalcanal, August 1942-February 1943* (Boston: Little, Brown & Co., 1949); and John Miller, Jr, *Guadalcanal: The First Offensive* (Washington, DC: Historical Division, Department of the Army, 1949), one of the many useful volumes in *The United States Army in World War II, The War in the Pacific* series.

21. Bix, *Hirohito*, 460–62; Hayashi, *Kōgun*, 58–66.

22. Willmott, *The War with Japan*, passim. Willmott concludes "If one refuses to accept that Japan's defeat was assured from the time that its carrier aircraft struck at the U.S. Pacific Fleet at its base at Pearl Harbor on 7 December 1941, then it was in the first two years of the Pacific War that the basis of America's victory and Japan's defeat was established," *The War with Japan*, 159.

2

Losing the War

Japanese leaders knew that they would be at a tremendous disadvantage in any lengthy war with the United States. Asked for Japan's chances in a war with Americans in the Pacific, Admiral Yamamoto expressed confidence in Japan's military capabilities in the short term but could make no prediction about the long run. In his oft-quoted phrase:

> If I am told to fight regardless of consequence, I shall run wild considerably for the first six months or a year, but I have utterly no confidence for the second and third years.[1]

Historians sometimes read into the second part of Yamamoto's statement foreknowledge of Japan's inevitable and total defeat. A less ex post facto reading is that it refers more to the imponderables of protracted war than the exact nature of Japan's final defeat. War was an unpredictable business, and the success of Japan's long-term strategy was dependent on a number of imponderables. She first had to drive the western colonial powers from the Far East. Then, while integrating the newly captured resource areas into the empire's core industrial base, she had to sustain an extended modern war and bring the China Incident to a successful conclusion. Careful preparation of in-depth defenses and stalwart resistance by the emperor's warriors would make any enemy approach to the Home Islands so difficult and costly that a peace settlement recognizing Japan's historical right to hegemonic power in Asia could then be negotiated. That, at least, was the plan, and, after Japanese forces ran wild in one of the most brilliant and well-executed military campaigns in history, the first part had been successfully accomplished.

But the rest of the war still had to be fought, and its ultimate outcome would be heavily determined by how well Japan used her initial advantage to fight it. A recent historian of the early Pacific War has argued that the root of Japanese defeat lay in the fact that the Imperial Army and Navy simplistically assumed that they could fight the Pacific War in the manner they were prepared and wanted to fight it. When from mid-1942 the United States refused to play by Japanese rules and instead began to fight the war on her own very different terms, Japan was doomed.[2] There is much to be said for this argument, but what it ignores is that Japan did not even fight the war she herself had planned to fight. Neither overexpansion on the Outer Perimeter nor the risk of the carrier arm at Midway were necessary parts of her original strategic plans. At a time when the United States might have welcomed an opportunity to shut down the Pacific theater, these moves triggered an increased Allied commitment to the region and provoked the Japanese high command to commit major forces to a debilitating attritional struggle on the enemy's terms in the Solomon Islands and New Guinea. If Japan had more faithfully followed her original strategy, a less vigorous American response and a more careful preservation of Japanese air and naval power would have given a very different strategic face to the Pacific War in 1942.

From the beginning of its modern nationhood, Japan's most important grand strategic imperative had been the protection of the Home Islands and the imperial polity. Commodore Perry's visit had never been forgotten, and besides providing resources, space, populations, and investment opportunities thought necessary for a rapidly growing empire—a kind of Japanese Manifest Destiny—the acquisition of Korea, Formosa, the Mandates, Manchuria, and positions in China all served the purpose of creating an impenetrable territorial defensive buffer around Japan. Hence the army's concern with the size and quality of the Kwantung Army in Manchuria and, after the elimination of the Imperial Russian Fleet, the navy's ambition for parity with Britain and America, the only other naval powers that could pose a threat to Japan.

In 1914 Japan proper was probably as safe from direct attack by her immediate neighbors as any nation at that time could have been. But the development of new weapons during and after the Great War—particularly submarines and warplanes—created novel strategic problems. The German strategy of unrestricted submarine warfare had come close to tipping the balance of war in favor of the Central Powers, and Japan, heavily dependent upon maritime imports and exports, would clearly be vulnerable to sustained submarine attacks. An even greater direct threat was posed by the interwar development of the long-range bomber. Though the effectiveness of strategic bombing had not yet been thoroughly tested, operations in Western Europe from 1939 had clearly demonstrated the destructive effect of massed bomber attacks on urban areas. From their own extensive terror bombing in China, the Japanese knew exactly how vulnerable the lightly constructed, densely settled cities on the Asian continent were to attack from the skies. It was clear that the great urban areas of Japan would be equally vulnerable to damage and conflagration inflicted by enemy warplanes.

The submarine and warplane, then, added new and more complicated dimensions to the traditional threats of armies and surface fleets and provided the military with obvious incentives to extend Japan's control of the sea lanes and expand the boundaries of her air spaces. The same weapons that threatened Japan, however, also presented new military opportunities. Their integration into conventional forces served as force multipliers, allowing Japan to project her military power over the entire Far East, far beyond the directly adjacent areas already incorporated into the greater Japanese industrial economy. By 1941, the southern resources that Japan so urgently needed were in reach militarily in a way that would have been impossible two decades earlier.

Gaining the periphery in early 1942 fulfilled Japan's immediate military goals. The new territories greatly increased the size of the buffer zone that separated Japan proper from her enemies. Their resources increased Japan's ability to fight a sustained war. But they also added new and strategically vulnerable areas to the expanded periphery of the empire. The traditional Japanese theaters of war in Manchuria, China, and the surrounding seas had all been located within an operational radius from Tokyo of about 1,250 miles. The acquisitions of 1941–1942 more than doubled this radius of action while tripling the areas to be defended by Japanese forces. The move to the south also took Japanese forces to some of the most rugged and isolated places in the world. East of the Indies and within ten degrees of the equator, this enormous territory consisted entirely of impenetrable landmasses, disease-ridden coasts, and tiny and widely separated atolls and islands of the tropical sea. The area contained only small and primitive human populations, no large settlements, no developed facilities, and precious few natural resources.[3] Every bullet, can of food, pound of rice, roll of barbed wire, and drop of oil used by Japanese forces would have to come from within the empire along extraordinarily long lines of communication. Protection of the heart of the empire from attack, even perhaps its very survival, would depend upon the defense of these new and far-flung places. Loss of these territories would expose the new rich resource areas in Southeast Asia, themselves located at great distances from the homeland, to attack. If these were cut off from the industrial core of the empire, it would mean the war was lost. In Vaubanian terms, the outworks had suddenly become strategically irreplaceable parts of Japan's main fortifications.

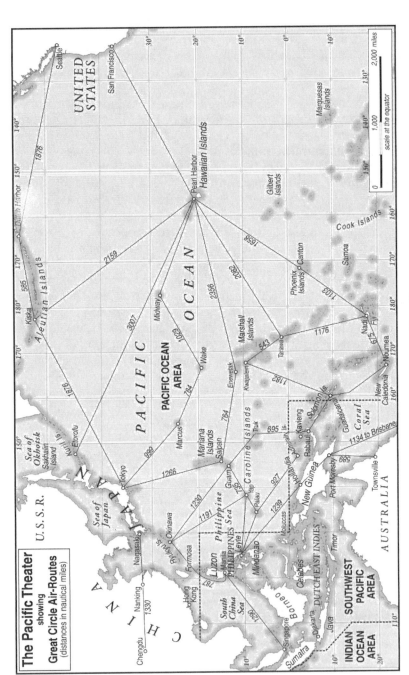

Map 2.1.   Pacific Theatre: Distances. *Source:* U.S. Navy Hydrographic Office.

From the beginning, therefore, Japanese strategy in the Pacific was predicated on organizing a perimeter defense that could hold the Allies off while the new resource areas were fortified and integrated into the wartime economy. Operations like Midway, Guadalcanal, and Port Moresby could be viewed in this context as attempts to expand the defensive perimeter in order to deny forward positions to the enemy. But these "victory disease" objectives all turned out to be impossible to take or to hold on to. The disaster at Midway crippled the Combined Fleet's carrier arm. At Guadalcanal, Japanese airpower had to operate at its absolute maximum range from Rabaul, which allowed only minutes over the target. The navy inflicted a series of costly defeats on the American fleet and managed to land two divisions of infantry there, but it was not enough to recapture the island. Once Henderson Field was fully operational, Japanese warship and transport-cargo ship losses reached unsustainable levels. Makeshift attempts to use nighttime runs by fast fleet destroyers and submarines also led to heavy losses and never delivered adequate supplies to Japanese forces on the island.[4] It proved similarly impossible in Papua New Guinea to sustain Japanese forces over the Owen Stanley Range against Fort Moresby. Every mile that the Japanese advanced only drove the enemy back on its main forces and resources. Poor logistics caused more Japanese soldiers to die from starvation, disease, and lack of rudimentary medical care than were killed by the enemy. Once the Allies established sufficient airfields, they began a multicolumn advance that culminated in December and January with the capture of Japanese strongholds in the Buna-Gona area, thereby clearing the extreme northeast coast of New Guinea. By the end of 1942, the fierce battles in the seas around the operational areas had so used up the unexpectedly vulnerable carrier forces of both sides that establishment of land-based airpower became even more critical. Throughout 1943 the struggle would continue to capture, defend, or develop successive points from which land-based aircraft could provide air cover for shipping, naval, and amphibious operations.[5]

The Japanese did not fail to respond to their late 1942 setbacks. In December Imperial General Headquarters (IGHQ) ordered the evacuation of Guadalcanal, which was accomplished by early February. A new Army-Navy Central Agreement called for Japanese forces to occupy and secure strategic points in the Solomons north of Guadalcanal and on the upper northeast New Guinea coast around Lae and Salamua. From Rabaul, air and naval attacks on Allied bases in the Solomons were to continue. Another central agreement in March declared the attainment of a superior and impregnable position in the southeast area of "vital importance to the strategic national defense of the homeland." Priority was to be given to building up key points on New Britain and in New Guinea and to intensify defensive efforts in the Solomons and Bismarcks. Reinforcements poured into the area.[6]

Despite these efforts, the slow but relentless Allied advance on Rabaul, the linchpin of this part of the national defense zone, continued. By November 1943 Admiral Halsey's forces, operating from Guadalcanal, had advanced up the Solomon chain as far as Bougainville, eliminating or bypassing Japanese garrisons along the way while capturing or building airfields to support each new operational step forward. MacArthur's Allied air forces gained air superiority over the northern New Guinea coast and set out to destroy Japanese airfields, bases, and lines of communication while his ground forces used amphibious operations and airdrops to seize key points or maneuver around isolated Japanese garrisons. By the new year, Allied forces had reached the Cape Gloucester-Saidor area, virtually completing the outflanking of Rabaul.[7]

The Japanese had fought fiercely when they were able against this onslaught but before their defensive strong points could be finished or their airfields made operational, they had either been taken, bypassed, or isolated. Rear zones with little defensive preparation suddenly became the front lines. By late 1943 Japanese forces, especially her air and naval strength, had been terribly eroded. Clearly the strategy of forward perimeter defense that had been employed since 1942 was losing its effectiveness even though the material balance between the two adversaries during this period was still fairly even. Despite a growing submarine menace in home waters, the southeast Pacific was the only part of the empire's perimeter defenses that seemed seriously at risk. It was dawning on IGHQ, the navy, and even the army that the Pacific had become their most critical theater and the one in which victory or defeat would be decided.

Clearly something had to be done before Japan's Pacific defensive perimeter became hopelessly compromised. An Imperial Conference in September 1943 issued a "General Outline of Future War Direction" that represented a major shift in Japan's conduct of the war. Calling for resolute measures to build up a decisive military capability, especially in airpower, the "Outline" ordered preparation by mid-1944 of an Absolute National Defense Sphere running the line Kuriles-Bonins-Inner South Seas-Western New Guinea-Sunda Islands-Burma which was to be held at all cost. Forces in the Solomons, Admiralties, and northeast New Guinea were to continue to resist while strong points and operational bases were established farther back. Any deep enemy penetration would be met with concentrated forces sallying from the Philippines. In the central Pacific, reinforced outposts in the Gilbert and Marshall Islands were to hold out as long as possible into 1944 while the Carolines and Marianas were being made defensible.[8] Fanatical resistance by the remaining Outer Perimeter garrisons would allow Japan to trade space for time while her new defenses were being readied. Unfortunately, the new Absolute Defense Sphere was to be overrun before it was ever completed.

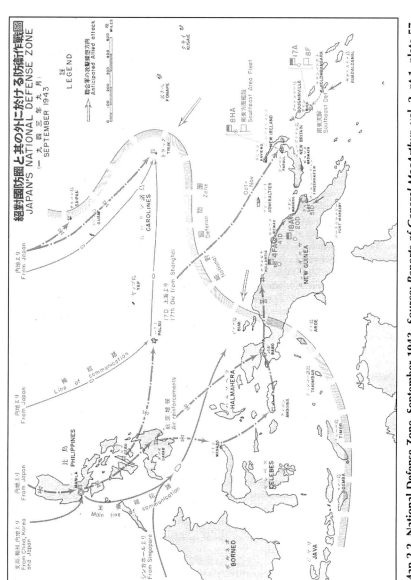

Map 2.2 National Defense Zone, September 1943. *Source: Reports of General MacArthur, vol. 2, pt.1, plate 57.* Department of Defense, 1950.

Once they had curtailed the Japanese advance in 1942, the Allies methodically began seizing forward positions, engaging and destroying Japanese air, naval, and, where necessary, ground forces, while developing the logistical apparatus for a future full-scale attack on Japan. At the same time they launched a submarine offensive to destroy Japan's merchant fleet and cut her off from the resources needed to run her wartime economy and supply her armed forces. But there were also limitations to what the Allies could do. Well into 1943, shortages of shipping, men, equipment, and logistical capability in the southwest Pacific often limited the American advance more than Japanese resistance. At Pearl Harbor, the Pacific Fleet, its carrier units almost depleted in the battles of 1942, would not be ready for large offensive naval operations in the central Pacific before late 1943, when newly produced warships and their recently trained crews would begin to arrive.

But at the end of 1943, just as Japan was attempting to rejuvenate her Pacific defenses, the Americans, having decided to bypass Rabaul, finally launched an accelerated two-theater offensive that the Japanese were not yet ready for and could not stop. In the southwest Pacific, MacArthur's forces raced to the western end of New Guinea by July 1944. Under this assault, successive Japanese lines of resistance crumbled and finally had to be pulled back to the Indies. The Philippines were invaded in October, providing the U.S. Navy in the process with the opportunity to sink most of the remaining major surface units of the Japanese Fleet at the battle of Leyte Gulf. Despite fanatical resistance and the introduction of Kamikaze tactics, IGHQ's hope to make the Philippines the site for a decisive showdown with the United States had failed. The ensuing liberation of the Philippines from Japanese control allowed Allied planes to join their submarine brethren in the attack on merchant shipping, and by early 1945 virtually all the Japanese convoy routes had collapsed, completing the isolation of the southern resource areas from Japan.[9]

Meanwhile, the U.S. Fleet under Nimitz had begun its parallel central Pacific offense. It moved rapidly through the Gilbert and Marshall Islands in late 1943 and early 1944, reduced Truk and other isolated bases to harmlessness with massive carrier raids, and in July captured the Marianas, within B-29 range of Japan, destroying the remainder of Japan's operational carrier force and its naval airpower in the battle of the Philippine Sea. After clearing the Palaus and supporting the invasion of the Philippines, Nimitz's carriers rampaged through the seas around Japan and the Marines successfully assaulted Iwo Jima in February 1945. From these forward positions, the Americans enforced a virtually complete air and sea blockade of the Home Islands and carried out the destruction of Japan's cities by strategic bombing. While fighting in the Philippines still raged, IGHQ proclaimed a new ne plus ultra National Defense Zone running along the Chinese coast to Formosa, the Ryukyus, and Japan herself. But this new Inner Zone was itself breached when the Americans landed on Okinawa, securing it by August despite fanatical Japanese resistance and attacks by thousands of suicide planes.[10] As the Americans prepared to invade Kyushu in November and Honshu the following spring, when Allied forces released from Europe would have completed their transfer to the Pacific, the Japanese military began girding itself and the nation for a last decisive battle on Japanese soil.[11]

Why, after the fall of 1943, had American forces been able to move so rapidly into the empire? A recent history of the war ascribes this success primarily to the ability of the U.S. command to adapt more quickly, flexibly, and effectively to strategic opportunities than the Japanese, even before the material balance between the two sides became lopsided. It is true that the Americans after late 1943 held an increasing quantitative and qualitative material superiority. But even before then, they utilized surprise, concentration of force, and overwhelming airpower to advance against selected strategic points when and where they wanted, subject only to logistical constraints. By fighting on ground of their own choosing, they managed to avoid, bypass, and isolate major concentrations of Japanese forces and to conduct amphibious landings against little or light initial resistance while relentlessly moving their airfields forward. This was done, moreover, with amazing economy of force. Not until the invasion of the Philippines and Okinawa did landings on a European scale take place, and the vast majority of conquests were made with small forces, seldom more than two, and often less than a single division, forces of a size that routinely disappeared daily on the Eastern front.

Despite the initial slowness of their advance, then, from late 1942 the Allies enjoyed a continuous string of ever more complete military victories. The American Navy won all but one of their engagements with the Imperial Japanese Navy after Guadalcanal. All seventy-two army and marine amphibious landings in the Pacific succeeded. By late 1944, U.S. submarines owned the sea lanes and her land and carrier-based planes ruled the sky. How else to interpret the rapid advance of U.S. forces in 1944–1945 as other than undeniable evidence that the total collapse of Japanese defenses and the catastrophic end to the Pacific War was preordained and inevitable?

Along these lines historians have often taken the Japanese to task for their long-term defensive strategy. The time gained by their initial onslaught was not used effectively to organize their war effort or to construct the kind of interlocking, in-depth defenses behind the Outer Perimeter combat zone on which the survival of the empire would rest. Instead Japan squandered two years, a significant portion of her fleet, and most of her trained land-based and carrier airpower for no true strategic purpose. When the Americans came on in 1944, the Japanese were neither ready nor capable of stopping them.

Still, it is easy to forget how unique the struggle in the Pacific was. Not since ancient times, perhaps, had opposing great powers had to adapt so quickly to the novel problems of amphibious warfare on such a colossal scale. There was no obvious textbook solution to the challenges the Japanese faced in properly organizing a successful defense of their historically unprecedented military position, and the plans and actions of both sides would constantly have to be adjusted to new situations and unforeseen factors.

Like the Japanese, the Allies also had to fight the war, for it was the fighting that would determine victory or defeat. Despite the eventually overwhelming nature of the Allies' victory, not until near the end of the war did the United States have a clear timetable and fully developed plan for the defeat of Japan. Some of this initial uncertainty was because the defeat of Germany was given priority, and plans for the destruction of Japanese forces became tied to the date of German surrender. Early war planning had called for the total defeat of Japan by 1948. After the first year of war in January 1943, the Casablanca Conference approved increased pressure in the Pacific, and the following August the Quadrant Conference gave permission to bypass Rabaul and initiate a double advance into the empire, adopting as a goal the defeat of Japan within twelve months of Germany's defeat. But there was no overall blueprint, and the Philippines, Ryukyus, Formosa, and Malaya were tentatively targeted for 1945, with final operations against Japan proper to begin in 1947 and extend into 1948. By late 1943 planners concluded that, even assuming the defeat of Germany by October 1944, there was no prospect of defeating Japan by October 1945. It was only the immense success of the renewed American advance from late 1943 onwards, especially the simultaneous seizure of western New Guinea and the Marianas by the summer of 1944, that enabled following operations like the invasion of the Philippines to begin several months ahead of schedule. And as late as the Hiroshima bomb, the final invasion of Japan was planned to begin only in the spring of 1946. The wide variation in the projected dates for Japan's demise well illustrates the often uncertain progress of the Pacific War. U.S. mediation of Japan's defeat was contingent upon, among other things, the conduct and outcome of the war in Europe and the North Atlantic, the secondary status of the theater, the level of military resources committed, production schedules, extreme logistical problems caused by distance and shipping shortages, and lack of service facilities, not to mention the ferocious resistance, strategy, and countermoves of the Japanese themselves.[12]

In assessing the course of the Pacific War, we should also emphasize that against great odds Japan somehow managed to sustain her war against the Allies for a not inconsiderable time span—three years and eight months— about the length of the American Civil War. It is sometimes forgotten just how late in the war it was before Japan proper was directly touched by war's destruction. Unlike Germany, which endured some three and one half years of round-the-clock bombing, the destruction of Japanese cities had only really gotten underway with the first great B-29 incendiary raid in March 1945—some forty months after Pearl Harbor. And it was only in April of that year that Japanese military leaders began to seriously consider even the most minimal steps toward ending the war. Even in August, Japan, though beaten, remained a very dangerous foe. The armed forces still had millions of soldiers and sailors under arms and occupied huge areas on the Asian continent. Thousands of planes, both operational and suicide, were held in readiness. The army, in particular, was prepared to fight on at any cost, and the looming American invasion of the Home Islands provided a welcomed opportunity for an honorable, if catastrophic, final battle.[13] The actual date of Japan's surrender, in August 1945, only three months after Germany's surrender, came as a kind of surprise, and certainly a relief, to those who expected to have to use the full weight of Allied arms against Japan well into 1946. That the final defeat of Japan took such a long, arduous, and uncertain road raises fundamental questions about the possibility of alternative outcomes and suggests that the pace, timing, and end date of the Pacific War may have been more malleable and changeable than is usually thought.

NOTES

1. There are many different renditions of Yamamoto's statement, that quoted is from Morison, *Rising Sun*, p. 46. Also Coox, "Effectiveness," 1–14.

2. H. P. Willmott, *The War with Japan*, p. 178, passim.

3. Eric Bergerud, *Touched with Fire: The Land War in the South Pacific* (New York: Viking, 1996), 53–118 and a companion description in his *Fire in the Sky: The Air War in the South Pacific* (Boulder, CO: Westview Press, 2000), 95–153. When Bergerud's book on naval warfare in the South Pacific appears, his trilogy will constitute the most complete and insightful current treatment on the war in the South Pacific. Also excellent on the logistical problems of the Allies are Robert W. Coakley and Richard M. Leighton, *Global Logistics and Strategy, 1940–43* (Washington, DC: OCMH, Department of the Army, 1955) and *Global Logistics and Strategy, 1943–45* (Washington, DC: OCMH, Department of the Army, 1968). The former is very revealing about the limits on the Allies' ability to send forces to the Pacific.

4. Works by Frank, Morison, and Miller previously cited. Frank's *Guadalcanal* uses both Japanese and Allied sources and is the best modern treatment. For an insightful, though not always convincing, treatment of the U.S. Marines in the Pacific, see Craig M. Cameron, *American Samurai: Myth, Imagination, and the Conduct of Battle in the First Marine Division, 1941–1951* (New York: Cambridge University Press, 1994), which covers much more territory than its title suggests. U.S. Marine Corps operations are covered in great detail in United States Marine Corps, *History of Marine*

Corps Operations in World War II, 5 vols. (Washington, DC: Historical Branch, Headquarters U.S. Marine Corps, 1958–71, 1968).

5. For the Buna campaign, *Reports of General MacArthur*, vol. 2, part 1, 124–217; Samuel Elliot Morison, *HUSNO*, vol. 8, *New Guinea and the Marianas* (Boston: Little, Brown & Co., 1953); Samuel Milner, *Victory in Papua* (Washington, DC: OCMH, Department of the Army, 1957). A good treatment of the difficulties of the Buna campaign and more revealing than the official histories is Jay Luvaas, "Buna, 19 November 1942–2 January 1943: A Leavenworth Nightmare," in Charles E. Heller and William A. Stofft, *America's First Battles, 1776–1965* (Lawrence: University Press of Kansas), 186–225.

6. Hayashi, *Kōgun*, 60–66.

7. Besides the *Reports of General MacArthur*, vol. 2, parts 1 & 2 and the official histories: Samuel Eliot Morison, *History of United States Naval Operations in World War II*, vol. 6, *Breaking the Bismark Barrier* (Boston: Little, Brown & Co., 1950); John Miller, Jr., *Cartwheel: The Reduction of Rabaul* (Washington, DC: OCMH, Department of the Army, 1959), recent histories of the war in the southwest Pacific area are Stephen R. Taaffe, *MacArthur's Jungle War: The 1944 New Guinea Campaign* (Lawrence: University Press of Kansas, 1998); Thomas E. Griffith, Jr., *MacArthur's Airman: General George C. Kenney and the War in the Southwest Pacific* (Lawrence: University Press of Kansas, 1998); and Edward J. Drea, *MacArthur's ULTRA: Codebreaking and the War Against Japan, 1942–1945* (Lawrence: University Press of Kansas, 1992). Gilmore's *You Can't Fight Tanks With Bayonets*, passim, is illuminating on Japanese morale.

8. Hayashi, *Kōgun*, 71–78; *Reports of General MacArthur*, vol. 2, pt. 1, 225–29.

9. For the war in the Philippines from the Japanese point of view, based on postwar interrogations, see *Reports of General MacArthur*, vol. 2, pt. 2; Samuel Eliot Morison, *History of United States Naval Operations in World War II*, vol. 12, *Leyte* (Boston: Little, Brown & Co., 1959); Robert R. Smith, *The Approach to the Philippines* (Washington, DC: OCMH, Department of the Army, 1953); M. Hamlin Cannon, *Leyte: The Return to the Philippines* (Washington, DC: OCMH, Department of the Army, 1954); Robert Ross Smith, *Triumph in the Philippines* (Washington, DC: OCMH, Department of the Army, 1963). The most recent treatment of the naval battle of Leyte Gulf is Kenneth I. Friedman, *Afternoon of the Rising Sun: The Battle of Leyte Gulf* (Novato, CA: Presidio Press, 2001); Richard Connaughton, John Pimott, and Duncan Anderson, *The Battle for Manila: The Most Devastating Untold Story of World War II* (Novato, CA: Presidio Press, 1995).

10. Samuel Eliot Morison, *History of United States Naval Operations in World War II*, vol. VII, *The Aleutians, Gilberts, and Marshalls* (Boston: Little, Brown & Co., 1951). The Marianas are covered by vol. 8 cited in note 5 above; Morison, *HUSNO*, vol. 14, *Victory in the Pacific* (Boston: Little, Brown & Co., 1960); Philip A. Crowl and Edmund G. Lowe, *Seizure of the Gilberts and Marshalls* (Washington, DC: OCMH, Department of the Army, 1955); Philip A. Crowl, *Campaign in the Marianas* (Washington, DC: OCMH, Department of the Army, 1960); and Roy Appleman, James M. Burns, et al., *Okinawa: The Last Battle* (Washington, DC: Historical Division, Department of the Army, 1948); James M. Burns, one of the authors of this latter history, among the first of the U.S. Army's volumes on the Pacific War to appear, is a long-term colleague at Williams College. The best recent treatment of Okinawa from

all sides, and required reading, is George Feifer, *Tennozan: The Battle of Okinawa and the Atomic Bomb* (New York: Ticknor & Fields, 1992). For an inside account from the Japanese side, see Colonel Hiromichi Yahara, *The Battle for Okinawa*, trans. Roger Pineau and Masatoshi Uehara (New York: John Wiley & Sons, 1995). One of the most illuminating studies of Marine amphibious warfare is Jeter A. Isely and Philip A. Crowl, *The U.S. Marines and Amphibious War: Its Theory and Its Practice in the Pacific* (Princeton: Princeton University Press, 1951). Osprey Publishing's Classic Battles and Campaign Series contains a number of recent, short, but useful histories of the campaigns of Nimitz's central Pacific drive. Written from both the United States and Japanese points of view, they constitute in many ways a complete history of the Marines' amphibious assaults across the Pacific: Derrick Wright, *Tarawa, 1945: The Turning of the Tide* (Botley, Oxford, UK: Osprey Publishing, 2001); by Gordon Rottman, *The Marshall Islands, 1944: Operation Flintlock, the Capture of Kwajalein and Eniwetok* (Botley, Oxford, UK: Osprey Publishing, 2004); *Guam 1941 & 1944, Loss and Reconquest* (Botley, Oxford, UK: Osprey Publishing, 2004); *Saipan & Tinian, 1944: Piercing the Japanese Empire* (Botley, Oxford, UK: Osprey Publishing, 2004); *Okinawa, 1945: The Last Battle* (Botley, Oxford, UK: Osprey Publishing, 2002); Jim Moran and Gordon L. Rottman, *Peleliu, 1944: The Forgotten Corner of Hell* (Botley, Oxford, UK: Osprey Publishing, 2002); and Derrick Wright, *Iwo Jima, 1945: The Marines Raise the Flag on Mount Suribachi* (Botley, Oxford, UK: Osprey Publishing, 2001).

11. Frank, *Downfall*, is the final word on the ending of the war, with close attention to the Japanese side as well as American strategic bombing, preparations to invade Japan, and the decision to drop the atomic bomb. Also useful is John R. Skates, *The Invasion of Japan: Alternative to the Bomb* (Columbia: University of South Carolina Press, 1994). For the strategic bombing campaign against Japan, there is the important and in some ways exhaustive United States Strategic Bombing Survey, *The Final Reports of the United States Strategic Bombing Survey*, part II, *The Pacific*. A guide to the Survey is Gordon Daniels, ed., *A Guide to the Reports of the United States Strategic Bombing Survey: I. Europe, II. the Pacific* (London: Offices of the Royal History and Society, 1981). The best recent history of the bombing of Japan is Kenneth P. Werrell, *Blankets of Fire: U.S. Bombers Over Japan During World War II* (Washington, DC: Smithsonian Institute Press, 1996).

12. The evolution of American strategy is covered in detail in Louis Morton, *Strategy and Command, The First Two Years* (Washington, DC: OCMH, Department of the Army, 1962); Maurice Matloff and Edwin M. Snell, *Strategic Planning for Coalition Warfare, 1941-1942* (Washington, DC: OCMH, Department of the Army, 1953); and Maurice Matloff, *Strategic Planning for Coalition Warfare, 1943-1944* (Washington, DC: OCMH, Department of the Army, 1958). Ross, *American War Plans*, cited previously, gives a clear overview of American strategic decisions.

13. What should be the final word on this period and these issues is Frank's *Downfall*.

3

Winning the War

By August 1945, Japan was a defeated and devastated country. The very totality of that defeat, in retrospect, makes her fate appear almost predetermined. Indeed, since the war, historians and participants on both sides have consistently argued that Allied victory in the Pacific was inevitable, and that therefore Japan's Pacific War was doomed to failure from the start. But was Japan's defeat inevitable? Could the war have had a significantly different course and outcome?

Alternative, or "what if" history has proven quite popular in recent years. Military history, with its drama and controversies, has been particularly well-suited to such counterfactual treatment. Certainly arguments about the "turning points" of the Pacific War have long provided grist for the mill of historical debate. What if the duty officers at Pearl Harbor had reacted differently to early morning radar sightings of approaching enemy planes? What if at Midway American dive-bomber pilots had not come upon the Japanese carriers at a uniquely vulnerable moment? Would the Leyte Gulf landings have failed if the captain of the super battleship "Yamamoto" had wreaked havoc on the helpless U.S. transports instead of turning back in the face of frantic antics by hopelessly outclassed American destroyers and escort carriers? Would torpedoing of the "Indianapolis" while it was carrying Little Boy to Tinian Island have delayed the use of the atomic bombs long enough that the invasion of Kyushu would have gone forward? Would the face of World War II, and therefore world history, have been changed if Japan had attacked the Soviets in late 1941, preventing the movement of Russian forces westward from Manchuria and allowing the Wehrmacht to capture Moscow? Replying or rethinking such events can be useful and revelatory as well as immensely entertaining.

Unfortunately, most counterfactual military histories tend to focus on individual episodes and to rely on dramatic reversals of fortune. But in dealing with a gigantic event like the Pacific War, individual episodes, no matter how dramatic, lose some of their unique explanatory value because they are themselves the product of many prior actions and events. It is instead the interaction and cumulative effect of a number of such striking individual episodes combined with thousands of prior and subsequent smaller actions and events that in the end determine a recognizable outcome. A compelling alternative history of the Pacific War must therefore provide a convincing analysis of the general systemic factors at work in such a huge and complicated event as the Pacific War and suggest how their spiraling synergies might have interacted in a different war to modify or change the war's outcome.

In our overview of the military course of the Pacific War, we argued against the often expressed notion that Japan's decision to go to war was some kind of reckless and voluntary national suicide. Everything in Japan's modern history and in the regional and world situation led her leaders to the conclusion that it was the proper and, in any case, unavoidable time to strike. We also showed how "victory disease" trumped an entirely rational initial plan to organize a defense in-depth for the empire in the Pacific, leading to overexpansion and premature attritional warfare on the Outer Perimeter. By the end of the first two years of war Japanese forces were so weakened, and her imperial defenses still so underdeveloped, that the Americans were able to penetrate successive, belatedly organized, National Defense Zones with relative ease, and bring the war directly to Japan proper.

During postwar prison interviews, former Army Minister and Prime Minister Tojo identified three factors as the main causes of Japanese defeat:

1. The American naval leapfrogging strategy, bypassing centers of Japanese power.
2. The far-ranging activities of the Fast Carrier Forces, Pacific Fleet.
3. The destruction of merchant shipping by U.S. submarines.

Tojo's analysis clearly located Japan's defeat as a Pacific defeat. His explanation went directly to the heart of Japanese military failure: no coordinated and effective defense of the empire was ever mounted. After 1942, Japanese forces were unable to prevent enemy amphibious assaults, carrier fleets, and submarines from penetrating, disrupting, and destroying Japanese defenses and lines of communication.

But the decision to go to war, the choice of opponents, and early war strategies also contributed to Japan's ultimately total defeat. The first two years of the war, especially, represented a major missed opportunity. Obviously, for Japan to have fought a more successful Pacific War, a different strategic engagement and direction of resources during that period was required. In fact, the elements for a more successful war effort did exist. Japan could have taken better advantage of her swift and overwhelming early victories over Allied forces in Southeast Asia and the Pacific. She could have managed her resources and military power so as to inflict significant reverses and substantial time delays on the Allied counteroffensive. At a minimum, she could have put off military defeat long enough to create a significantly different endgame that avoided total defeat and utter devastation.

At the highest levels of Japanese leadership there was certainly a general awareness that, after their initial successes, the main strategic problem they faced was how to construct an imperial defense and organize for protracted war. In March 1942, Prime Minister Tojo and the Chiefs of Staff submitted to the emperor a "General Outline of Policy of Future War." Its first two points stated that:

1. In order to bring BRITAIN to submission and to demoralize the UNITED STATES, positive measures shall be taken by seizing opportunities to expand our acquired war gains, and by building a political and military structure capable of withstanding a protracted war.
2. By holding the occupied areas and major communication lines, and by expediting the development of key resources for national defense; efforts shall be made to establish a self-sufficient structure and to increase the nation's war potential.

In an accompanying report they explained that:

It will not only be most difficult to defeat the UNITED STATES and BRITAIN in a short period, but, the war cannot be brought to an end through compromise.

It is essential to further expand the political and military advantages achieved through glorious victories since the opening of hostilities, by utilizing the present war situation to establish a political and strategic structure capable of withstanding a protracted war . . .

We deem it highly essential to constantly maintain resilience in our national defense, and build up the nation's war potential so we will be capable of taking the steps necessary to cope with the progress of situation.

If a nation should lose its resilience in national defense while prosecuting a war, and become unable to rally from an enemy blow; the result would be short of her desired goal, no matter what victory she might achieve in the process.[1]

But in the hectic and heady days of early victories and in the face of more immediate tactical challenges, the principles of mobilization for protracted war and organization of in-depth imperial defenses got pushed to the side. Energies went instead into overexpansion and then a continuous feeding of military resources into the Solomons and New Guinea. It was only after it became clear that the battle on the periphery had been lost that the high command began making a belated effort to build up new defending positions to the rear on which the enemy could exhaust himself. But these attempts to create successive lines of defense deeper within the empire failed, and always for the same reasons. The infrastructure of airfields and supply facilities remained inadequate and underdeveloped. Preparation of integrated defenses was started too late, and the forces allocated to them were too small. There were attempts to glean lessons from each failure and use them to prepare more effective resistance, but even the much more effective late war defenses continued to be compromised by incompleteness and shortages of combat troops. Because defense in-depth remained so incomplete and inadequate, the Americans were able to bypass or isolate major concentrations of Japanese strength and overwhelm specific targets despite the most desperate and suicidal efforts of their defenders. What could have changed this cycle of too little, too late? Even a casual examination of a map of the Pacific will reveal that the strategically irreplaceable points in any defense of Japan and her new acquisitions were the Philippines and the Marianas. From the Philippines, enemy forces could cut Japan off from her southern resources and conduct bombing campaigns against or invade the China coast, Formosa, and the Ryukyus. As long as the Philippines were held, Japan's strategic position in the south was secure. In the central Pacific the Marianas were Japan's last major bastion. Within very long bomber range of the Home Islands, they were the only position from which the Allies could mount a truly massive and effective strategic bombing campaign against Japan's cities and industries. As long as the Marianas were held, long-range destruction of Japan from the air would be impossible.

In mid-1942, then, the problem to be solved was not how to defeat a superior enemy at the end of an immensely long chain of communications, but rather how to organize the empire's inner defenses so that when the enemy penetrated through one of the unavoidable gaps in the outer defenses he could not go far or fast and would expose his forces to defeat. A more successful, perhaps even a war-winning strategy for Japan, would have:

1. Avoided "victory disease"
2. Built an effective in-depth National Defense Zone
3. Protected its merchant marine
4. Prevented strategic bombing
5. Maintained submarine attacks on the enemy's lines of communication
6. Denied the enemy air superiority
7. Kept a "fleet in being"
8. Forced more Okinawa-type battles on the enemy

9. Disrupted and delayed the U.S. assault schedule
10. Postponed the war's endgame until 1946–1947

All these goals were linked to one another in an interconnected sequence of self-reinforcing cause and effect. Even partial success in most of them would have gone a long way toward parrying the strategy and blunting the attacks of the Allies, thereby altering the face of the Pacific War. The first two goals, avoiding "victory disease" and building an in-depth National Defense Zone, of course, provide the fundamental basis for a better Japanese strategy. All the other goals flow from them. Protecting the merchant marine and preventing strategic bombing would enable Japan to produce the material required by protracted war well past the historical date of the collapse of Japanese industry. Submarine attacks against Allied merchant shipping would take advantage of the Allies' greatest vulnerability, particularly in the first two years of the war. Preventing the establishment of enemy air superiority would checkmate the Allies' greatest strength. Forcing more Okinawa-type battles would wear down the enemy's resources and morale. Keeping a "fleet in being" would provide the means for decisive counterattacks. The cumulative effect of these factors would have been a system that limited the exposure of Japanese forces, enabled them to fight at an advantage, and provided a firewall against enemy incursions. By delaying and perhaps even stopping the U.S. assault from 1943 to 1944, Japan would have positioned herself to negotiate a favorable peace settlement between 1946 and 1947, when Allied exhaustion and the developing Cold War would make unconditional surrender and the occupation of Japan seem less pressing.

At its most fundamental level, the establishment of a National Defense Zone meant the organization of defense in-depth: interlocking, overlapping, mutually supporting defenses that would delay the enemy and set the stage for concerted counterattacks by friendly air and naval forces. From the beginning, therefore, thickened defenses should have been constructed in the Philippines and on Saipan, Guam, and Tinian. Hundreds of airfields should have been prepared. Defenses of similar density and manpower would be constructed on Formosa, the Ryukyus, and the Bonins, completing an inner core of mutually supporting strong points which could protect the empire's vital lines of communication and prevent harm to Japan itself. In a nutshell, the empire's Pacific defenses should have been constructed outwards from the Home Islands rather than inward from the periphery.

Following this policy would have required an earlier and fairly significant shift of labor, material, and military forces to the Pacific front. Of course, it could be argued that this concentration on the Pacific would have simply weakened critical defenses on the other half dozen major fronts, leaving Japan open to defeat from a different direction than the Pacific. But it should be kept in mind that none of the other territories under Japanese control ever constituted a significant mortal threat to Japan. Allied forces in the China-Burma-India area were never strong enough to seriously threaten Japanese control of Southeast Asia and the Indies. The loss of Burma in 1944–1945 was the result of an entirely self-inflicted wound caused by a mentally unbalanced local commander over the protests of his subordinates. Only small forces were ever needed in the Dutch East Indies. The war in China, contrary to much that has been written, was not much of a burden after 1941. Chinese forces were regularly and easily defeated by any serious Japanese effort, the annual level of casualties was low, and rabid economic exploitation of the occupied areas proved quite profitable.[2] The China war, in other words, paid for itself as well as providing a large pool of "blooded" units that could be deployed elsewhere. American aid to China disappeared into the hands of a terminally corrupt Nationalist regime more interested in waiting the war out and hunting communists than in fighting the Japanese. The logistical expense of maintaining over-the-hump bomber operations in western China was a total misuse of Allied resources kept going by politics rather than military usefulness. Finally, until August 1945 the Soviets did not pose a threat to Manchuria. The Pacific, then, was the only theater that posed any real threat to the empire. If Japan was to be defeated, it would be in the Pacific that the fighting that determined the outcome of the war would take place.

But what about the immediate military situation in the Pacific in mid-1942? Would concentration on deep defenses have taken place at the expense of the direct and ongoing military struggle with the enemy farther to the south and east? There are a number of ways to answer this question. First, what did the fighting on the periphery matter if, as was actually the case, the enemy was eventually able to take the strategically indispensable inner positions because their defenses were unfinished, inadequate, and incapable of mutual support? Second, in-depth fortified positions would allow Japanese forces to take advantage of their central position and interior lines. Even while being established, they would serve as a well-equipped springboard and transit point for the development and/or reinforcement of hardened positions farther out, in western New Guinea, the Paulus, Yap, Rabaul, Halmera, Truk—forward positions that the enemy would have to attack in order to advance at all. Third, a strategy of defense in depth in the Pacific would have allowed Japanese forces to fight a smarter and more limited kind of delaying action on the extreme perimeter. Forces stationed on Tarawa, Kwajalein, the Solomons, and eastern New Guinea, would function only as expendable outposts, there to force the enemy to deploy his forces, and to harass and delay them, but not worth the risk of any major portion of Japanese strength. As the enemy advanced past these outposts, it would encounter hardened positions that were capable of defending themselves or contributing to the active defense of their neighbors. Having avoided tremendous naval and air attrition, massive numbers of planes from further back in the developed defense zone could easily be deployed forward along with the concentrated Combined Fleet to engage enemy landings and forces.

It might, however, be objected that a very much reduced resistance beyond the western New Guinea-Rabaul-Truk-Marianas line might have permitted an even more rapid American advance in the Pacific. Rather than clawing their way up the Solomons and along the northern New Guinea coast for almost two years, they would have arrived with little struggle or loss at the first substantial barriers of the new National Defense Zone. A straightforward answer to this objection rests on the very real limits under which the Allies were operating in the Pacific in 1942–1943. The Pacific Fleet, as we have noted, was not ready to begin its central Pacific drive before late 1943 and could lend only limited forces to expedite MacArthur's operations to the southwest. Recall also that it was all the Allies could manage to land and maintain in action a single Marine division on Guadalcanal in August 1942, a force commitment that was precipitated only by Japanese efforts to construct a forward airbase in an extremely sensitive area. The ill-fated, unsupported drive on Fort Moresby likewise triggered an earlier than desired commitment of Allied forces to Papua New Guinea. Throughout the rest of 1942 and into 1943, in fact, Allied forces were committed in a quite piecemeal fashion to the southwest Pacific Area of Operations, where relatively tiny forces defeated the Japanese in detail time after time. In fact, the speed of Cartwheel, the twin-pronged Allied advance on Rabaul, was limited more by logistical problems that would never be entirely corrected than by Japanese resistance. Finally, Papua New Guinea and the Solomon Islands were some of the most disease-ridden places in the world. Units committed to those areas were literally under a death sentence, primarily because of malaria, which quickly destroyed the effective strengths of the combat and support units of both sides. Indeed in these small encounters, Japanese attacks often took place because local commanders realized that even a short delay in action would quickly render their units useless.

For both logistical and medical reasons, then, it would have been difficult for the Allies to have speeded up their advance in the southwest Pacific in 1942–1943 even in the face of differently structured Japanese defense. By limiting their investments of forces into these forward outpost areas, the Japanese Army and Navy would have conserved their strength for more effective resistance in the deeper and more readily supplied defensive zone that was being constructed. Japanese warships, cargo vessels, and troopships would have avoided the heavy losses they suffered in 1942–1943 when they attempted to fight or to supply isolated forward garrisons so far from their own effective air cover. Japanese aircraft, instead of operating in a highly vulnerable and unforgiving manner hundreds of miles forward of their bases, could have been much more efficiently dedicated to protection of their airfields and lines of communication and to interdiction at fairly close range of Allied naval moves.

Certainly avoiding "victory disease" and building an effective National Defense Zone would have greatly enhanced Japan's chances in the Pacific War. Avoidance of premature and uncontrolled commitment of major forces to attritional battles for relatively insignificant strategic points, combined with the construction of in-depth defenses from the interior of the empire outward, would have paid enormous dividends. There was a crucial window of opportunity in 1942–1943 in which Japan's overall military position in the Pacific could have been strengthened. Once that window closed, belated attempts to create various ne plus ultra lines in 1944 failed because by that time the factors identified by Tojo—U.S. submarines, carrier task forces, and amphibious capabilities—had made it impossible to maintain a viable imperial defense in the Pacific.

Adoption of a different overall strategy with shortened and safer supply lines would have limited merchant shipping exposure to air attack—especially early in the war—and meant faster turnaround times and increased deliveries of material, equipment, and personnel. There were even greater advantages to be derived, as we will see, from more effective convoying and antisubmarine operations closer to home waters. It is not hard to imagine the integrated defenses that could have been developed on Biak or Pelieu or Leyte if those areas had been well stocked, armed, manned, and fortified in late 1943, supported by massive air forces deploying forward from similar strong points beyond the reach of the enemy, backed by the menace of a concentrated Combined Fleet. The second part of the book will explore just how these different elements could have contributed to a different and more successful Japanese strategy for fighting the Pacific War.

NOTES

1. Louis Morton, *Strategy and Command: The First Two Years*, 611–13.
2. A good history of the war in China is Edward L. Dreyer, *China at War 1901–1949* (New York: Longman, 1995) and for these conclusions especially, 306–11.

4

Missing Ships

The second volume of the *Reports of General MacArthur* features a brightly colored bar graph titled "Japan's Merchant Shipping Losses."[1] Plate No. 151, as it is labeled, is intended to demonstrate the single most important cause of Japan's defeat in the Pacific War: the destruction of her merchant marine by Allied forces. The vertical bars on the graph show the impact of the dynamic interplay between ship losses and new ship construction on the overall tonnage of the Japanese merchant fleet between December 1941 and August 1945. The red columns show that losses reached five hundred thousand gross tons per quarter in the winter of 1942–1943 and accelerated to one million tons per quarter or more in three of the four following quarters. Black columns show that new construction from Japanese shipyards during this period was not insignificant, reaching a level of several hundred thousand gross tons in the spring quarter of 1943 and peaking at five hundred thousand tons of new shipping in the summer quarter of 1944. But the increases in new ship construction never matched losses. From a beginning total of over six million gross tons, the graph's cascading blue columns show Japanese shipping reduced to less than two million gross tons by the end of the war. Total war losses, a majority caused by American submarines, came to 2,346 ships aggregating 8.6 million gross tons. Plate 151's impressive and dramatic portrayal of destruction thus illustrates a central truth about the Pacific War. But it obscures the fact that improvement in this dismal area of the Japanese war effort not only was possible but clearly could have significantly modified the outcome of the Pacific War.

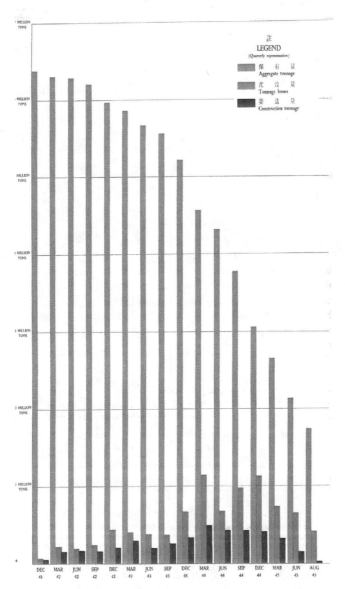

船　舶　損　耗　表
JAPAN'S MERCHANT SHIPPING LOSSES
(一九四一年十二月より一九四五年八月迄)
DECEMBER 1941–AUGUST 1945

註
LEGEND
(Quarterly representation)

保　有　量
Aggregate tonnage

沈　没　量
Tonnage losses

建　造　量
Construction tonnage

**Figure 4.1. Japan's Merchant Shipping Losses, 1941–1945.
Source:** *Reports of General MacArthur*, **vol. 2, pt. 2, plate 151.
Department of Defense, 1950.**

In December 1941, Japan had a modern merchant marine of approximately 6.4 million gross tons and civilian shipyards capable of adding another six hundred thousand tons of new construction per year. Prewar planning concluded that three million tons of shipping per year would suffice, though just barely, to sustain Japan's economy during the first two years of the war, though fuel supplies depended on the speed with which the newly conquered southern oil fields could be put back into production. But since on the eve of war, the navy and army together had already requisitioned some 3.7 million tons of shipping for military purposes, Japan began the war with a deficit of civilian shipping. It was hoped that once the early war needs of the army were met, the total amount of shipping under military control could be reduced to approximately 2.8 million tons, with the surplus transferred back to civilian usage.[2]

Japan therefore began the war with less than the absolute minimum tonnage that should have been reserved for the operation of the civilian economy. However, captures, new construction, lower than expected losses, and a steady reduction in army requirements brought the amount of shipping devoted to the civilian economy back up to the magic 3.1 million ton minimum in June, where it stayed through the end of 1942, and at a level never less than 2.9 million tons for the first ten months of 1943. The close calculations of prewar planners seemed to have come true. This success, however, was misleading. As Mark Parillo's study of the Japanese merchant marine during World War II so lucidly demonstrates, neither the Japanese government nor the navy had devoted much thought or planning to the wartime control and protection of the merchant fleet. The authority to direct shipping was divided among noncooperative navy, army, and civilian agencies. Responsibility for escorting and protecting shipping was even more dispersed among numerous naval districts with inadequate personnel and resources. Though in a general sense the navy was responsible for protecting shipping, the Combined Fleet nourished plans for decisive battle and withheld fleet units from escorting duties except for valuable military cargoes close to the combat zone. Since there was no central authority to organize convoy traffic, most ships sailed singly and without escort to and from their destinations. The units that were dedicated to the escorting of civilian, as well as many military cargoes, were scarce, technologically backward, and ill trained; aircraft devoted to antisubmarine warfare (ASW) were too few and too old. Lack of interest, centralized command, doctrine, and resources meant that the Japanese merchant marine was a disaster waiting to happen.[3]

That this disaster did not immediately manifest itself was due almost entirely to the fact that the American submarine offensive against Japanese shipping was not initially very successful. At the very beginning of the war, reversing a long-standing public position, the United States ordered immediate initiation of unrestricted submarine warfare against the Japanese. But the burden of attack in the Pacific fell on only about fifty American submarines—half of them obsolete S-type boats—and many of their prewar commanders turned out to be unfit for the rigors of actual submarine warfare. American admirals, who were after all just as attuned to the prospects of decisive battle as their Japanese counterparts, diverted much of this inadequate force to fleet operations and useless pursuits of fast enemy warships rather than concentrating on vulnerable Japanese shipping. The loss of operational Asian bases meant that U.S. submarines operating from Pearl Harbor or Fremantle, Australia, had to spend sizeable amounts of their time on patrols simply getting to and from the target areas. Finally, and most critically, American torpedoes suffered from multiple hidden mechanical flaws that regularly caused them to malfunction, and the Navy Bureau of Ordinance stubbornly refused to acknowledge the extent to which problems existed or to undertake any program to fix them. Local commanders finally pinpointed the sources of the problems, but it was not until September of 1943 that the mechanical malfunctions were entirely eliminated. It is no accident that the widespread provision of reliable torpedoes then coincided with a rapid escalation in sinkings.[4] Given the practically unfettered access to Asian shipping lanes, it is not impossible to imagine that reliable torpedoes, on their own, might have easily doubled or tripled submarine sinkings of merchant vessels during the first one and a half years of war. In a perverse way, it was unfortunate for Japan that more of her merchant marine was not sent to the bottom in 1942, for larger losses would have focused attention earlier and more rapidly on the underlying and potentially fatal deficiencies in her maritime protection policy.

It is not the case, however, that the Japanese were completely ignorant of the virtues of convoying or of the importance of escorts. Maritime district officers tried to assemble convoys and to provide some kind of escort for them when they could, and the services sometimes provided air cover for military or naval cargo moving to the front. Nor were Japanese ASW tactics totally ineffective—over the course of the war American submarines suffered a loss rate of about 25 percent.[5] But, even when convoys were organized, they were invariably very small—generally no more than four to eight transports and, often, a near equal number of escorts of varying speed and quality. They did not take advantage of the law of large numbers or the formulas governing adequate levels of escorting. Even later in the war, at a time when the Allies were routinely sending convoys of eighty to one hundred or more ships across the North Atlantic, Japanese convoys rarely consisted of more than twenty ships.[6]

As it were, Japanese ships steamed the maritime trade routes of Asia, often alone, and usually without proper escorts. Sinkings were so infrequent at first that there was no real cause for alarm. But by late 1942, sinkings of military transports in the Solomons and the central Pacific helped push losses to a level of one million tons per year compared to the prewar annual replacement rate by new construction of six hundred thousand tons. By the last quarter of 1943, losses had accelerated to a quite alarming rate of 1.8 million tons per year, three quarters due to submarine attacks. In 1944, as the enemy began to add massive aircraft strikes to their campaign against shipping, the loss rate doubled to 3.8 million tons per year. By the end of 1944, Japan's merchant marine was reduced to 40 percent and by August of 1945, 23 percent of its prewar level.[7] Most of the shipping that nominally remained was severely damaged, inoperable, or confined to harbor. After February 1945, when U.S. submarines had run out of targets, three quarters of continuing losses were due to air attack or aerial mines. Japan's war production capacity was reduced to nil.

Whence had come this enormous maritime disaster? Simply put, the Americans had gained valuable experience, fixed their torpedo problems, greatly increased the number of modern, radar-equipped boats on patrol, and cleverly used broken Japanese codes to direct their boats to their targets. All of this came together in late 1943 and was magnified in 1944 by carrier raids and the establishment of Allied air bases deep within the empire.[8]

In response to this growing menace, in late 1943 the Japanese finally took action. A centralized convoy system was organized. More escorts were produced or converted from small craft. Air surveillance was increased. ASW minefield barriers were laid in narrow southern passages, the Kuriles, and southwestward from Kyushu down the Ryukyus to the China coast. Production priority was shifted to merchant ship construction, especially tankers, and new construction jumped to 1.1 million gross tons in 1943—twice the prewar estimated maximum—and then to 1.6 million tons in 1944. At one point the emperor himself intervened to enforce coordination of shipping and resolve service differences. But it was all too little, too late.[9]

Japan's ability to wage war was fundamentally dependent upon the ability to transport massive amounts of raw and semi-finished materials to the Home Islands and from there finished war materials to the Pacific front lines. Beginning in late 1943 it became increasingly difficult, and by early 1945, impossible to transport by sea.[10] Any number of deficit factors—the limited size of the prewar merchant marine, the lack of escorts, interdepartmental and interservice uncooperativeness, technological backwardness, and limited shipyard capacity—can be cited to make the downward curve of accumulating losses so colorfully presented in Plate 151 seem an almost natural, unchallengeable process, preordained, inevitable, and irrevocable. But early war failure to institute effective maritime protection was not peculiar to the Japanese. With even less reason than Japan—given their extensive experience in World War I—the Allies exhibited similar delay, resistance, and incompetence in organizing the protection of their own merchant marines. The main difference was that the Allies overcame their confusion and mistakes quickly enough to limit their shipping losses to an acceptable level, and Japan did not.

This outcome could have been much different. Changes in timing and organization could have significantly slowed the pace of the degradation of Japan's maritime capabilities, and this would have paid enormous dividends in the mid and late war period. Japan could not, of course, totally prevent losses to U.S. submarines and aircraft. The answer to the problem of submarine campaigns against shipping—a comprehensive system of escorted convoys—was widely known at the beginning of the war. Before the British organized their convoy system in World War I, unrestricted warfare by German U-boats seemed well on its way to inflicting so much damage on her merchant marine that Britain could not continue the war. Once convoying was introduced, the U-boat menace was rapidly reduced to manageable proportions.[11]

Why in both world wars was there resistance by all the protagonists to convoys? The principal reason was fear that convoying would reduce flexibility and turnaround times compared to individual ship sailings. Even if they were fully loaded and ready to sail, individual ships had to delay their departures while waiting for the convoy to assemble. Once they sailed, convoys had to steam at the speed of their slowest ships. Unlike single sailings, convoys needed escorts, and conservative admirals were reluctant to denude the battle fleet of its own destroyer type crafts for escort duties. It was also feared that convoys would do the U-boats' work for them by periodically concentrating their targets in large groups rather than seeking safety in hundreds of individual sailings widely and unpredictably spread out across the vastness of ocean. Instead of diluting their strength by escorting widely separated convoys, navies preferred to concentrate their assets in ASW groups designed to hunt submarines in the open sea and kill them before they could attack vulnerable shipping.

Counterintuitive as it might have been, however, convoys were a true war-winning tactic. By their very nature, convoys empty the sea of ships. Instead of individual ships sailing in every quadrant of the map, concentration in convoys meant that most areas of the sea contained no targets at all. The key was to avoid enemy submarines, if at all possible, and experience showed that even without escorts, convoys dramatically cut losses. Large convoys were particularly effective. They extended scarce escort resources by concentrating them in sufficient numbers to protect large numbers of ships. In World War II, indeed, it was calculated that the larger the convoy the better because slight increase in the size of the circumference of a convoy allowed room for significant numbers of additional transports without requiring a similar proportional increase in the number of escorts.

Though much safer than individual sailings, convoys could not always evade the enemy. With the advent of radio, a picket submarine could be used to discover and track a convoy while vectoring multiple attackers into its path—the origins of so-called wolf packs. But even if losses from interception were heavy, a large enough convoy meant that large numbers of ships would still get through. And in the meantime, convoys which had not been intercepted could steam without losses through the areas left uncovered by concentrations of U-boats elsewhere.

Convoys, moreover, though designed to avoid the enemy and provide safety in numbers, also played an important offensive role in the maritime battle by creating ideal conditions for escorts to attack and destroy the hunters. Submarines by nature are hard to detect, but the development of acoustical gear and depth charges—and later planes and radar—made it possible to pursue a boat even after it submerged. The ships of the convoy, then, acted as bait to draw submarines close enough to the escorts to be sunk. In both world wars, despite disastrous beginnings, the Allies, by adopting an escorted convoy system, were able to first frustrate, and then punish the U-boats to such an extent that they had to be withdrawn from action.

This was not, however, the case in the Pacific in World War II, though it might have been, for the extent and nature of the expanded Japanese empire would have lent itself well to the establishment of a centrally controlled convoy system. A glance at a map of wartime shipping routes shows that the Japanese merchant marine would spend its time on long voyages bringing resources from the southern areas to the factories and workshops in the Home Islands. Converted to war material, those resources would then return by the same routes along the Asian mainland to the south, or by way of Saipan and the Palaus, to Truk and Rabaul in the central and southern Pacific.

As map 4.1 shows, the westward advance of Allied forces had by mid-1944 forced the abandonment of routes east of the Philippines. But routes to the west of the Philippines, in the Indies, along the Asian coast, and across the inland seas remained viable far longer. This provides grounds for rethinking Japan's maritime defense strategy, because for most of the war the economically important shipping routes were out of the range of enemy aircraft and her submarines were forced to operate in totally hostile waters thousands of miles from their bases. The area contested by commerce raiders was analogous in size to the North Atlantic. Bounded by land on all sides, with long stretches of shallow but navigable coastal waters and narrow channels of approach from outside except to the northeast, this *mare nipponaise* enjoyed a number of defensive advantages. Its multiple routes were well known and charted. Its weather patterns were generally milder

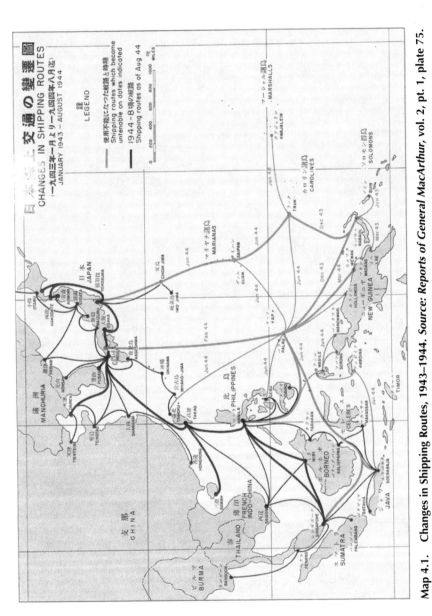

Map 4.1.   Changes in Shipping Routes, 1943–1944. *Source: Reports of General MacArthur*, vol. 2, pt. 1, plate 75. Department of Defense, 1950.

and more predictable than the Atlantic. Unlike the Atlantic, hardly any of its waters were beyond the reach of patrolling airplanes. In Singapore, Manila, Hong Kong, Shanghai, and Tokyo, the Japanese merchant fleet had access to some of the greatest harbors in the world.

What might the earlier adoption of a large convoy system along the corridors of East Asian seas have meant for the Japanese war effort? Japan's maritime defeat naturally lends itself to counterfactual analysis, for almost any other outcome we could imagine would be an improvement on the historical case. Based on Allied experience in the Atlantic we know that the loss ratio of convoyed to individual ship sailings was 1 to 2.5. In other words, switching from individual sailings to convoys alone reduced ship losses by 60 percent. Assuming that this ratio can be applied to the Pacific, and that starting in 1942 one half of total Japanese merchant tonnage had been organized into large convoys, we can estimate the impact on Japanese shipping that adoption of convoys could have had during the war. This result, shown in table 4.2, can be compared to the actual war losses in table 4.1.[12] The counterfactual model predicts that the adoption of convoying by the Japanese would have prevented the loss of some 2.7 million gross tons of shipping over the course of the war. Compared to the historical result, where tonnage fell to 93 percent of prewar at the end of 1942, 77 percent at the end of 1943, and 40 percent at the end of 1944, the counterfactual model predicts 92 percent of prewar tonnage left at the end of 1943, 74 percent at the end of 1944, and 65 percent (or almost three times the historical 23 percent) in August of 1945. Now, according to prewar calculations about the Japanese economy during wartime, it was estimated that one gross ton of shipping could—on average—transport twenty gross tons of cargo over the course of a year.[13] By this measure, losses from Japan's neglect of convoying cost her over the course of the war around fifty-three million tons of cargo moved. That is enough freight to have sustained the civilian sector of the Japanese wartime economy for an entire year. Therefore, *by*

Table 4.1. The Japanese Merchant Marine, 1941–1945 (Gross Tonnage)

Date	Additions	Losses	Net Change	End of Period Total	Index
12/7/41				6,384,000	100
12/41	44,200	51,600	−7,400	6,376,600	99
1942	661,800	1,095,800	−434,000	5,942,600	93
1943	1,067,100	2,065,700	−998,600	4,944,000	77
1944	1,735,100	4,115,100	−2,380,000	2,564,000	40
1/45–8/45	465,000	1,562,100	−1,097,100	1,466,900	23
Total					
8/14/45	3,973,200	8,890,300	−4,917,100	1,466,900	23

Source: Parillo, *The Japanese Merchant Marine in World War II,* 1993

Table 4.2.   The Japanese Merchant Marine:
The Counterfactual Case, 1941–1945 (Gross Tonnage)

Date	Additions	Losses*	Net Change	End of Period Total	Index	Tons Not Sunk
12/7/41				6,384,000	100	
12/41	44,200	51,600	−7,400	6,376,600	99	
1942	661,800	767,100	−105,300	6,271,300	98	329,000
1943	1,067,100	1,446,000	−378,900	5,892,400	92	620,000
1944	1,735,100	2,880,600	−1,145,500	4,746,900	74	1,235,000
1–8/45	465,000	1,093,500	−628,500	4,118,400	65	469,000
Total 8/14/45	3,973,200	6,238,800	−2,265,600	4,118,400	65	2,654,000

*Assumptions: Starting in 1942, assume one-half of total tonnage in convoy with historical losses reduced by 60 percent (based on Allied experience in both world wars of a convoyed-to-unconvoyed ship loss ratio of 1:2.5).

itself, the adoption of convoying would have been worth an extra year of war production. Its overall impact would have been to move back the effective date of Japan's mercantile collapse by at least a year.

But even if it seems clear from our model that earlier adoption of a large convoy system along the corridors of East Asian seas would have meant a significant reduction in Japanese shipping losses, several arguments against this line of reasoning could be made. Historically, we know that the extensive organization of convoys that began in late 1943 coincided almost exactly with an increase in sinkings. It could be argued, then, that Japan's concentrating of shipping into convoys actually led to higher rather than lower losses to submarines. But, in fact, any correlation between Japan's organization of convoys and increased shipping losses is spurious. For one thing it flies in the face of a large body of other historical evidence about the actual experience of convoys under ferocious attack in the Atlantic. For another, to the end of the war Japanese convoys remained too small to have produced benefits or sufficiently decreased losses. The upswing in sinkings after the organization of convoys was caused by increased numbers of U.S. submarines on patrol, the replacement of defective torpedoes, and the increasing vulnerability of military and naval transports to air attacks.

It could also be argued that the cracking of Japanese codes by U.S. intelligence would have guaranteed the eventual destruction of her merchant marine. In particular, intercepts of the so-called water transport code—the radio code used to communicate with merchant ships and which they used to report their noontime positions—were systematically read by the Allies and used to vector enemy submarines to their victims. Given the transparency of their shipping movements—which the Japanese authorities refused to recognize—one could argue that U.S. submarines would always have been able to find and sink Japanese ships whether they sailed alone or in convoy. Besides the fact that Japanese security breaches could have been solved fairly easily and that it completely overlooks the "empty seas" and "safety in number" aspects of convoying, this objection does not take into account the second fundamental advantage of convoying: deliberately drawing enemy subs to the convoy where they can be engaged and sunk by escorting vessels and planes. Rather than the easy pickings of a sea filled with vulnerable, unescorted single ships, submarines would instead have to fight their way through an adequate number of well-armed escorts concentrated into a relatively few great convoys. Submarines, after all, were very fragile craft, and even with the inadequate ASW equipment arranged against them U.S. submarines suffered heavy losses in the Pacific. So, it is not too far a reach to imagine that the earlier adoption of a system of regular, escorted, large convoys might have enabled the Japanese merchant marine to have navigated with reduced losses, especially in dangerous areas like the east coast of Japan or to have turned the Luzon Strait, the Americans' "convoy college" into a "submarine cemetery." Under such a system, in fact, a certain amount of positional transparency might have actually been desirable. The enemy would figure out where the convoys were, but the convoy's escorts and shadowing planes would also know where the submarines had to be, greatly simplifying the task of destroying them.

A final objection to this line of reasoning might be that even though American submarines finally were responsible for a majority of all sinkings, by the end of the war the Allies could deploy many other lethal weapons against Japanese shipping. In the last few months of the war, in fact, Allied planes and aerially delivered antiship mines had surpassed submarines as the main causes of sinkings.[14] Therefore even improved defenses against submarines would not, in the end, have prevented the destruction of Japanese shipping. But this overlooks the fact that nonsubmarine losses near the end of the war were the coup de grace to an already inert shipping system, not the fatal blow. As a matter of fact, in those last months there were almost no targets left for U.S. submarines to attack because the remnants of the merchant fleet had been driven from the sea lanes into inactivity in harbors where they sat uselessly, easy targets for aerial borne bombs and mines.

That earlier organization of a viable convoy system would have significantly reduced merchant marine losses seems highly probable. Besides reducing losses from submarines during the first two years of the war, a well-organized convoy system would also have quickly created its own efficiencies, notably the treatment of all ships as part of a single pool, and the institution of an organized triangular route which eliminated ships sailing in ballast only. Earlier implementation of an organized system of escorts and air cover would have also provided invaluable experience with which to assess and prepare for the Allied submarine onslaught that began in earnest in late 1943. Even after the Americans solved their torpedo problems and increased the numbers of their submarines on patrol, large convoys, by their very nature, could have been expected to keep losses in check. Above all else the integration of significantly increased aerial cover for convoys—so decisive for the Allies in the Atlantic—could have paid large benefits.

But adoption of a large-scale convoy system, though it would have brought many benefits, would not in and of itself have won the war for Japan. For one thing, U.S. submarines would not have gone away, and from midwar on there were more than two hundred American submarines available for war patrols in the Pacific. Furthermore, after 1943 American advances allowed deployment of additional means of destruction against Japan's merchant marine. But no maritime protection system, after all, operates in a vacuum, and it would have been the combination of convoying with other factors that would have truly made a difference. In this case, the chances of survival of a viable merchant marine—along with all the additional production and transportation capacity that this implies—would have been immeasurably enhanced by the avoidance of "victory disease" and the organization of an in-depth National Defense Zone (NDZ), as suggested in previous chapters. Both would have reduced shipping losses: in the case of perimeter operations, by limiting exposure of military transport in overextended operations, and in the case of the NDZ, by building convoy protection into a defense in-depth from which land-based ASW planes could constantly blanket the surrounding waters with patrols. Furthermore, since the whole point of a different defensive strategy was to delay the Allied advance and deny them easy capture of key strategic points deep within the empire, denial of airspace would have postponed the day when Allied warplanes could bomb and mine at will. From an ASW point of view, this would also gain more time for the creation of strategically placed mine barriers.

In his penetrating study, historian Mark Parillo stresses the historical importance of the destruction of Japan's merchant marine and its contribution to Japanese defeat:

> In both aborted production and strategic immobility, the failure to protect maritime transport translated into decreased military force and a lessened ability to resist the relentless pressure of the Allied offensives. The destruction of the merchant marine hastened Japan's surrender, but by how much will always be a matter of some conjecture. The evidence suggests that a delay of six months to a year is probably not unrealistic.[15]

Certainly our counterfactual analysis would support this conclusion. A better job of protecting shipping by convoying could have postponed the collapse of Japan's wartime economy, and therefore her military defeat, for at least another year, and, as Parillo also argues, probably have forced postponement of the American invasions of the Marianas and the Philippines to 1945 and subsequent operations into 1946.[16]

If this had indeed been the case, then in the summer of 1945 Japan would not have been a defeated nation. Her merchant marine would still be operating at a viable level, her cities would be largely intact, and her war industries producing near to the 1944 level. Her numerous soldiers, well armed and supplied, dug deep in hardened defenses, would have awaited the coming American assaults with confidence, knowing that they would give as good as they got, and that their heroic resistance might indeed save Japan from humiliating and total defeat.

NOTES

1. *Reports of General MacArthur*, vol. 2, pt. 2, 620.

2. *Reports of General MacArthur*, vol. 2, pt. 1, 44–50, for prewar planning. The final word on Japanese shipping, and the source I have relied on heavily for this chapter, is Mark P. Parillo, *The Japanese Merchant Marine in World War II* (Annapolis, MD: Naval Institute Press, 1993); especially pages 32–38 and 74–83 for the contest between civilian and the services' needs. Another very useful, though massive source for Japan's maritime losses is the Joint Army Navy Assessment Committee, *Japanese Naval and Merchant Shipping Losses During World War II By All Causes* (Washington, DC: Navy Department, 1947), usually abbreviated as *JANAC*, on which most postwar estimates of Japanese losses rest.

3. Parillo, *Japanese Merchant Marine*, 63–73.

4. For faulty U.S. torpedoes: Keith M. Milton, *Subs Against the Rising Sun* (Las Cruces, NM: Yucca Tree Press, 2000), viii–ix; and in general the lively accounts of James F. Calvert, *Silent Running: My Years on a World War II Attack Submarine* (New York: John Wiley & Sons, 1995), 51–56, 156–57; and Charles A. Lockwood, *Sink 'Em All. Submarine Warfare in the Pacific* (New York: E. P. Dutton & Co., 1953), 20–22, 75, 85–86, 88–89, 111–14, 164; Lockwood was in overall command of U.S. submarine forces in the Pacific; and Peter Padfield's *War Beneath the Sea: Submarine Conflict During World War II* (New York: John Wiley & Sons, 1998), 338–54. Padfield covers submarine warfare in all theaters of the war and provides a useful comparative perspective on the different national submarine services.

5. See *United States Submarine Losses: World War II* (Washington, DC: Office of the Chief of Naval Operations, 1963) for a listing.

6. Parillo, *Japanese Merchant Marine*, 94–124 and especially 125–45.

7. Table A.8. "Size of the Japanese Merchant Fleet During World War II," Parillo, *Japanese Merchant Marine*, 242.

8. On the broken codes, Parillo, *Japanese Merchant Marine*, 84–93.

9. Parillo, *Japanese Merchant Marine*, 115–17, 133–39. For the emperor's role, 72–73.

10. Maps of disappearing routes in Parillo, *Japanese Merchant Marine*, 126, 144; Plate 75, "Changes in Shipping Routes, January 1943–August 1944," *Reports of General MacArthur*, vol. 2, pt. 1, 306, reproduced as map 4.1 in this chapter.

11. Parillo, *Japanese Merchant Marine*, 99–100, 115–16.

12. Actual losses from table 4.1 in Parillo, *Japanese Merchant Marine*, 292. For the final destruction of the Merchant Marine and its impact on the Japanese war effort, 203–21.

13. That is, three million tons could transport sixty million tons of cargo over the course of one year.

14. Parillo, *Japanese Merchant Marine*, 195–202; Werrell, *Blankets of Fire*, 231–33.

15. Parillo, ibid., 226.

16. The title of his last chapter: "Paths Not Taken," Parillo, *Japanese Merchant Marine*, 222–33, esp. 227–32.

5

Sunk

At the beginning of the war, expectations for the Japanese submarine service—the Sixth Fleet—were quite high. Japan entered the war with a large and technically advanced submarine fleet. The newest of her boats, especially the I-series of fleet and patrol boats, had incredible endurance, were fast on the surface, employed advanced optics, and were armed with excellent torpedoes that did not malfunction. Their officers and crews were all volunteers and the elite of the navy.[1]

For the attack on Pearl Harbor, the submariners were assigned a role second only to that of Japanese carrier aircraft and on December 7 twenty-eight I-boats, divided into several groups, were in Hawaiian waters. One group had reconnoitered ahead of the attacking carrier task force while another was positioned to intercept any enemy warships approaching from the east. Other groups were poised and ready to ambush ships trying to enter the base, pass between the islands, or retreat to the mainland. Five boats carried midget submarines whose task it was to penetrate the Pearl Harbor anchorage and cause as much damage as they could.[2]

The carrier attack on Pearl Harbor was devastatingly successful. But its companion submarine offensive failed miserably. All five of the midget submarines were detected and destroyed within hours of launching. A photograph of one of the battered midget submarines washed up on the beach became one of the lasting images of the war.[3] The I-boats, though suffering no significant loss on that day or in the following weeks on station around Hawaii, failed to find or sink anything of military value. Two-thirds of the entire Sixth Fleet, including twenty of its twenty-two operational ocean cruising boats, had been committed to the Hawaii operation. They came home having accomplished nothing except to alert the nervous Americans to their lurking presence by their radio transmissions.[4]

The submariners' next failure came in June, at Midway, where picket lines of I-boats totally missed the movements of the American carriers and failed to provide vital information about their presence to the main fleet.[5] Then, in August, after the Americans had landed on Guadalcanal, most of the Sixth Fleet's strength was committed to the struggle in the southwest Pacific. In late 1942 there were twenty, and by January 1943, thirty-eight boats in the area. They had some success against American warships but hardly bothered the accompanying merchant convoys at all.[6] The emperor, refusing to abandon isolated or bypassed Japanese Army garrisons, ordered the Sixth Fleet to divert a large number of submarines to clandestine supply and rescue missions far behind Allied lines to troops who would otherwise have been left to their fate. Submarine commanders strongly protested this misuse of their boats but could not oppose a direct imperial order.[7] Submarines could carry so little cargo or personnel, however, that in terms of its impact, these efforts were to be little more than a symbolic gesture. Nevertheless, over the course of the war, the army and navy would build more than fifty transport submarines for this purpose. Over the next year, as southwestern and central Pacific waters grew increasingly thick with Allied escorts, planes, submarines, and PT boats, Japanese submarines continued to be lost at a high rate—twenty on resupply missions alone.[8] When the American central Pacific drive began at Tarawa in October, things got worse. Nine boats were committed to the Gilberts: six were lost. Twenty-two boats were committed to the Marianas and the battle of the Philippine Sea in mid-1944: fourteen were sunk. In all of 1944, despite the addition of forty-four new boats, fifty-six were lost. Symbolically enough, in June, Admiral Takeo Tagaki, Commander of Sixth Fleet, trapped on Saipan with his headquarters, died leading his surviving staff in a banzai charge against invading American infantry. By October 1944, after the battle of Leyte Gulf the Sixth Fleet was finished, for all practical purposes, as a conventional submarine force.[9] Costly attempts to supply isolated and bypassed troops continued until the end of the war, but frustrated naval officers, like their counterparts in the air forces, began promoting suicide tactics. From late 1944 fleet boats not already serving as supply vessels were utilized to deliver human torpedoes— the *kaiten*—against ships in enemy anchorages, with very limited results.[10] In 1945, as the battle for the Home Islands began to loom, hundreds of smaller coastal defense boats, with a range of but one thousand miles and two torpedoes, were produced, none of which ever saw action. At the end, only twenty-one of the 149 full sized boats that had begun, or had been produced during the war, survived.[11] The contrast with the U.S. silent service—whose destruction of Japanese shipping made such an essential contribution to Japan's defeat—could not have been more stark.

The locations, and agents, of destruction of its boats speak volumes about the death of the Sixth Fleet. A total of thirty-six boats were lost in the Solomons-South Pacific-New Guinea area, two thirds in 1942–1943. Forty-one were lost in the central Pacific, all but four before 1945. Nine were lost in the Philippines in 1944–1945 and twenty-one in home waters, seventeen in 1945 alone. Throw in six boats lost in chilly Aleutian waters, and we have accounted for 113 of 130 total lost. In terms of the agents of destruction, one hundred of the 130 boats lost were sunk by Allied surface escort vessels (58 percent) or submarines (19 percent). Only fourteen boats were lost to direct air attack alone—half in 1945.[12] Obviously, most Japanese submarine losses came in close proximity to enemy naval units in contested waters. Submarine attacks on well-escorted American carrier and battleship support groups, invasion fleets, and alert and well-defended fleet anchorages were extremely dangerous. And as the war progressed, Allied code breakers began moving ambush units into the paths of patrolling Japanese submarines, which accounts for the large number lost to U.S. submarines operating in the antisubmarine warfare (ASW) mode. It is worth noting that almost no boats were expended in attacks on the long and vulnerable enemy lines of communication beyond the immediate war zone from Seattle to the Panama Canal.

Allied and postwar accounts of the defeat of the Japanese submarine service often focus on technology. Whatever their adequacy by international standards in 1941, the technical weaknesses of Japanese submarines soon were exposed in the hard school of American ASW warfare. The large I-class submarines were slow to submerge and once underwater were hard to maneuver. They had relatively shallow maximum diving depths, and their size made them easy to track under water on sonar. Their lack of climate control led to rapid crew exhaustion and reduced efficiency. But their greatest problem was lack of radar, which was universally adopted for use in American vessels in 1942, while Japanese boats began receiving primitive sets only in the fall of 1944.[13] Radar, of course, enabled escorts or planes to fix the position of surfaced submarines even in darkness or bad weather and played a critical role in Allied successes in the Atlantic as well as the Pacific. In its absence, Japanese submarines had to operate most of the war without adequate aircraft warning systems and to rely entirely on conventional optics instead of electronically fixing the location of enemy surface vessels. Japanese fire calculators—the instruments that provided the correct settings to speed torpedoes to a moving target—therefore had to work with often inaccurate visual sightings instead of precise electronic data. American calculators, by contrast, had grown so sophisticated by the end of the war that, even while submerged, boats could use periscope mounted radar to guide attacks against targets that could not be located by any other means. The Japanese did strive to install a whole series of technical upgrades in their submarines and by the end of the war had made major strides in developing antiacoustical external surfaces, surface radar, snorkels, and advanced submarine designs, including an innovative series of boats capable of very high submerged speeds, which were closely studied by the Americans after the war. But they never managed to catch up with the constantly evolving American ASW technology or produce the new design boats in sufficient numbers.

Such technical inadequacies go far toward explaining the potency and success of Allied ASW. Yet technical issues ultimately were not as important as Japanese Navy doctrine itself in limiting the effectiveness of Japanese submariners. Despite the obvious successes of German campaigns against merchant shipping in both world wars, the role assigned to Japanese submarines was purely offensive: to seek out and attack the warships of the enemy main force. In prewar plans for a decisive fleet engagement, in fact, pickets of submarines were expected to inflict a rather precise attrition rate of 30 percent on the U.S. surface fleet as it advanced westward from Pearl Harbor. The Navy General Staff and Combined Fleet's rigid insistence that submarines be subordinated to fleet operations and used in a direct combat attack role against enemy warships meant that submarines were viewed entirely in a tactical and reactive rather than a strategic way. In response to each Allied move, they were hastily thrown into battle in picket lines whose positions were constantly being shifted in response to daily or even hourly reports of enemy activity, wearing down equipment and men and exposing the boats to detection and destruction by Allied ASW. This offensive mentality was not entirely confined to the Japanese Navy—the United States also misused much of its submarine force in similar operations early in the war. But despite many efforts to change the minds of the navy brass, the primary mission of the Sixth Fleet—cooperating in battle with the main battle fleet—was never abandoned, and as American ASW improved, it became nearly suicidal. Yet as long as there were operational boats left, they continued to be sent out on increasingly hopeless operations against well-escorted enemy warships.[14]

Indeed, given the growing disparity between American and Japanese technology and capabilities, it is hard to see how the Sixth Fleet could ever have survived for long as a viable conventional combat submarine service, much less a war-winning strategic weapon. Japanese submarines, for example, could have done little to stop or retard the remarkable outpouring of U.S. ships and escorts from shipyards as well as the technical maturation of American ASW from 1943 on. The German Navy, after all, threw more than a thousand U-boats at the problem and also failed. To expect a victory in this arena might have been demanding too much. The magnitudes involved were, over time, just too insurmountable.

Nevertheless, there was a window of opportunity during the first year of the war in which Japanese submarines could have made a crucial contribution to Japan's war but did not. For as astonishing as it may seem, the Japanese submarine service never made a serious or sustained attack on American merchant shipping in the Pacific, even early in the war, when the Allied position in the Pacific was still uncertain, its supply lines most vulnerable, its maritime resources stretched to the absolute limit, and its ASW, although potent, did not yet hold an insurmountable edge over Japanese submarines.

Certainly the Americans knew that this window existed and were puzzled that Japanese submarines never took advantage of it. After the first months of war, no U.S. ship was fired on by Japanese submarines in and around Midway and Pearl Harbor. Vice Admiral Charles Lockwood, the principal architect of American submarine warfare against Japan, recounted the impact of the sinking by a Japanese submarine in October 1944 of a single U.S. merchant ship about halfway between San Francisco and Hawaii:

> . . . A shipping raid on our home waters, after almost three years of inactivity along that line, was a surprise indeed. The disturbance it caused, and the consequent dislocation of traffic, showed just how much the enemy could have embarrassed us by more of the same.[15]

Consider the quandary in which the Americans in the Pacific found themselves in early 1942. There were simply not enough merchant ships available to fight two major enemies across two great oceans at the same time. New ship and escort production was still largely on the drawing boards, most neutral shipping had long before been hired by the British, and most surplus ships under the American flag had already been taken under U.S. military control before Pearl Harbor. Furthermore, the decision to defeat Germany first meant that priority had to be given to the Atlantic. Even though the U.S. Navy and Admiral King always considered the Pacific the navy's war and deployed most of its resources there, from the point of view of merchant bottoms, servicing the U.S. war economy and fighting Germany made the Pacific the third choice in the commitment of mercantile assets. Like the Japanese, however, the Americans also had to transport every man, bullet, ration, and quart of oil they used in the Pacific. And because distances were longer, port facilities absent or inadequate, and American forces more scattered, ship turnaround times were a great deal slower. Compared to the Atlantic, for example, it took a ship two and one half times longer to move cargo to its destination in the Pacific; the loss of a single ship there had the impact of three ships sunk in the Atlantic. The maritime routes of the Pacific, moreover, lent themselves well to ship hunting. Along North America, the Pacific coast had very few natural anchorages or suitable major harbors. Most cargo traffic from the west coast to the war zone originated through one port—San Francisco—or, if coming from the Atlantic, through the Panama Canal. Destinations were equally few: Pearl Harbor, Australia, and a few islands in the south Pacific. American logistical operations, then, were funneled along predictable ocean routes. And though there was a great deal of ocean to hide in, the immense distances involved prolonged the time that ships were exposed to enemy submarines. Furthermore, aerial surveillance of U.S. waters was still rudimentary and escort vessels were rare.

The authors of the best recent history of the imperial Japanese submarine service concluded that:

> Immediately after the Pearl Harbor attack, the Japanese navy should have concentrated all ocean-going and fleet-type submarines in Hawaiian waters and off the U.S. mainland. . . . The large submarines ought to have been rotated systematically, and these two war patrol areas (Hawaii and the U.S. west coast) should have been maintained at least through 1942. That is, one-third of the available submarines should have been on station, one-third en route, and one-third being refitted. . . . While manning these two patrol areas, the submarines could have obstructed quite effectively the flow of American reinforcements being rushed westward, and at least in the early part of 1942, they would have been ideally situated to attack American warships en route to the U.S. mainland for permanent repairs after suffering damage during the Pearl Harbor attack.[16]

Japanese submariners were hardly blind to this opportunity. From the beginning of the war there was criticism within the service of its exclusive use as a direct combat arm against enemy warships, and calls for the strategic use of its boats against enemy merchant shipping. After the failure at Pearl Harbor, for example, the submarine service reported:

> The Hawaiian defenses are very sound and the enemy ships in general very much on their guard, making it impossible for submarines to enforce a blockade or cut the lines of communication. Enemy anti-submarine vessels kept up a relentless pressure and although our submarines did sight a few targets, they were counterattacked before getting a chance to put in their own attack . . . The submarine is a weapon for attacking merchant ships, i.e., its main function is commerce destruction."[17]

The few times that Japanese submariners were allowed to operate against enemy lines of communication, they compiled a decent enough record: early in the war off the Australian coast, for example, or, most notably, in the Indian Ocean in 1942–1943, where a few I-boats operating from Penang sank or damaged close to one hundred Allied ships aggregating several hundred thousand gross tons. Even their German ally, aware of its own success in the Atlantic early in the war, urged the Japanese to initiate a submarine offensive against American lines of communication in the Pacific. But such voices were either ignored or overruled, and actual attempts to mount such attacks were aborted in midstream by the naval command's insistence that submarine operations remain subordinate to fleet operations or tied down to clandestine supply operations. At last, in 1943, in response to the often harsh criticism of its submarine commanders, the navy issued a New Submarine Doctrine that for the first time recognized communications destruction as an important part of their mission.[18] But since by then there were not enough boats left after fleet or resupply operations to mount such operations, the reshaped doctrine was never put into effect.

American maritime vulnerabilities aside, there remains the question of why we should expect a Japanese submarine offensive against the American merchant marine to have been more successful than the Sixth Fleet's other failed operations during 1942. Happily, there is contemporary historical data that bears directly on this question. After the formal entry of Germany into war with the United States, Admiral Doenitz launched successive waves of aggressive U-boats against shipping off the east coast of North America and later the Gulf of Mexico and the Caribbean. For months the United States refused to organize its shipping into coastal convoys or to impose blackouts on seaboard cities. What followed was a slaughter of merchantmen long remembered by German submariners as the "happy days." Before they were finally withdrawn in August following the completion of the belatedly organized American coastal convoy system, the U-boats—never more than five on station at a time—sank well over four hundred ships exceeding two million gross tons. A handful of submarines, in other words, by a timely attack on unprepared merchant ships in virtually unprotected waters, had an immediate and negative impact on American maritime resources and war production.

One must therefore conclude that an even larger scale early-war submarine offensive off the west coast, at a critical stage in the military buildup in the Pacific, might have produced similar results, even if only temporarily, and influenced the long range calendar of the war. Every single transport used in the Pacific was a valuable and nearly irreplaceable asset. Loss of even a few freighters in 1942 would have greatly hampered an American buildup that even in August 1942, was having difficulties maintaining part of a single marine division on Guadalcanal. Several lucky torpedo hits—the sinking of a transport carrying an entire infantry regiment, a tanker full of high octane aviation fuel, or a ship loaded with engineering equipment and service troops—had the potential to completely throw off the Americans' calendar or to limit their immediate reaction to Japanese moves. Even simply forcing the Americans into a premature adoption of a massive convoy system might, over the short run, have slowed the speed of the American buildup.

So there was an early war window of opportunity to attack the Allied Achilles heel—the long lines of communication that ran east of the Hawaiian Islands and south of Seattle all the way to the South Pacific. Japan started the war with forty-two I-boats and added thirteen more during 1942. This was a sufficient number of fleet and patrol type boats to launch and for a time at least maintain a submarine offensive on the sea lanes that connected the U.S. mainland with the Pacific war zones. Even if each boat had sunk only two freighters before being sunk itself, it would have been worth it, for at that point in the war the Americans simply could not have replaced their losses.

A Japanese submarine offensive against American shipping, then, could for a time have brought the Allied buildup, at least as far as offensive purposes go, to a standstill. But the main thrust of this argument is not to make a dramatic or incredible claim about the war-winning potential of the Japanese submarine service. In war, timing is everything, and in this case the key is the timely threat of an offensive against Allied shipping in 1942, more than expectations of a massive and ongoing destruction of shipping. Like a jujitsu blow that produces its effect by its placement rather than brute force, a Japanese submarine offensive could have had a psychological impact all out of proportion to its actual material results. Of course American reaction would have eventually ended this moment of vulnerability. In a matter of months, certainly less than a year, Japanese long-range raiders would have met the same fate as the German U-boats. But in the meantime the Japanese would have gained what they needed most: the delay of the Allied counteroffensive in the southwest Pacific and time to establish the in-depth defenses within their NDZ.

At some point the Sixth Fleet would have had to curtail its antishipping attacks on the distant Allied lines of communication and pull its surviving boats back to home waters. Would this have been the end of the wartime usefulness of Japan's submarine service—its last hurrah, so to speak? Absolutely not, for the submarine offensive could have continued at a reduced but still dangerous level. Even if losses of I-boats had been heavy in 1942, twenty-five new attack boats would come into service during 1943–1944. This was enough boats to launch periodically a series of smaller scale, selective long-range attacks on American shipping designed to keep U.S. forces off balance and force them to devote even more of their resources to blanket escort duties in rear areas. The commencement of U.S. carrier task force raids in 1943 would have also provided new targets. But rather than trying to assault the swift and well-protected carrier groups themselves, the I-boats should have concentrated on the huge and more vulnerable American fleet trains upon which the fast groups depended for fuel, supplies, and replacements during their unprecedented long stays at sea. As U.S. forces advanced deeper into the empire, the sizeable fleets of freighters and auxiliary craft moving forward from supply bases in abandoned rear areas would also have presented lucrative targets.

Also important, though often overlooked, is the crucial contribution submarines could have made to Japan's own antisubmarine defenses. Except to the northeast, enemy submarines had to approach the waters that touched the Asian mainland through relatively narrow straits or across seas of moderate size. American submarine patrols, whether they operated from Freemantle or Pearl Harbor or were making a patrol from one to the other, had to pass through at least one and sometimes several of these choke points. Many of these passageways were suitable for mining, which had some success against transiting American submarines, as did constant ASW surface patrols. For American submarines, the danger and anxiety of getting through these passages to the hunting grounds and back ranked only behind that caused by a determined and accurate depth charging. A different use of Japanese submarines could have made it even more difficult.

Japan's RO-series boats, smaller and shorter ranged than I-boats, but more nimble, were perfectly adequate for this task. Taking advantage of the inner topography of the empire, they could have haunted the shallow waters off the Asian coast or the numerous relatively narrow passages between Malaysia, the Indies, Borneo, and the Philippines in search of enemy submarines. Dedication of the thirty-eight RO boats that came from Japanese shipyards during the war to the elimination of enemy submarines in transit would surely have paid dividends in the ASW contest. After all, there was only one confirmed sinking of an American submarine by a Japanese submarine over the course of the war, though American submarines were responsible for the sinking of twenty-five Japanese submarines.[19] This 25:1 disparity highlights the potential usefulness of submarine hunting by submarines. Since American submarines operating in the Pacific sank on average about six enemy ships during their active patrolling life, each one sunk by Japanese boats could potentially prevent the destruction of some thirty thousand gross tons of Japanese shipping. Submarines assigned in teams to guard specific passageways and to hunt or ambush U.S. submarines in the narrow or shallow approaches to the economically important trade centers could have been a potent addition indeed to the airplanes and surface vessels engaged on ASW in the NDZ.

To sum up, a submarine campaign against American shipping in 1942 was not only technically possible but also dreaded by the enemy. It would have been well worthwhile incurring heavy losses of Japanese I-boats—perhaps even the entire inventory of such boats—in order to disrupt and therefore delay the American buildup in the Pacific for a few precious months at an absolutely key moment in the war. As the war proceeded, the remaining I-boats should have operated against the most vulnerable shipping of Allied rear areas, rather than on fleet or resupply missions. Dedication of the service's RO boats to hunting and destroying U.S. submarines as they passed through navigational choke points on their way to attack the Japanese merchant marine, besides elevating the American loss rate, might have also helped to preserve a significant chunk of Japanese shipping. In the overall scheme of things, any or all of these measures would have made specific and significant contributions to the delay of the Allies and the defense of imperial maritime traffic. Given the undistinguished war record of Japanese submarines, almost any outcome other than the historical ones would have been an improvement.

NOTES

Borrowing the title of the earliest firsthand war memoir in English by a former Japanese submarine officer: Mochitsura Hashimoto, *Sunk. The Story of the Japanese Submarine Fleet, 1941–1945,* trans. E. J. M. Colegrave (New York: Henry Holt and Co., 1954).

1. The best and most comprehensive history of the submarine service, based on Japanese as well as American sources, is Carl Boyd and Akihito Yoshida, *The Japanese Submarine Force and World War II* (Annapolis, MD: Naval Institute Press, 1995), 8–35 for technical descriptions of Japanese boats, 36–38 for torpedoes. I have relied heavily on Boyd and Yoshida for the information in this chapter. See also a trilogy of books from the Naval Institute Press: Hansgeorg Jentschura, Dieter Jung, and Peter Mickel, *Warships of the Imperial Japanese Navy, 1869–1945,* trans. Anthony Preston and J. D. Brown (Annapolis, MD: Naval Institute Press, 1970); Erminio Bagnasco, *Submarines of World War II* (Annapolis, MD: Naval Institute Press, 1977); and Dorr Carpenter and Norman Polman, *Submarines of the Imperial Japanese Navy* (Annapolis, MD: Naval Institute Press, 1986).

2. Boyd and Yoshida, *Submarine Force,* 58–65.

3. For the midgets, Boyd and Yoshida, *Submarine Force,* 59–65; photo on 60; and Richard O'Neill, *Suicide Squads: The Men and Machines of World War II Special Operations* (Guilford, CT: The Lyons Press, 1999, 2000), 29–36.

4. Boyd and Yoshida, *Submarine Force,* 58. Firsthand descriptions of this and many other submarine operations in Hashimoto, *Sunk,* passim.

5. Boyd and Yoshida, *Submarine Force,* 77–84.

6. Boyd and Yoshida, *Submarine Force,* 92–107.

7. Hashimoto, *Sunk,* 97.

8. Boyd and Yoshida, *Submarine Force,* 113–27. For the role of submarines in supply efforts, Parillo, *Japanese Merchant Marine,* 173–94, esp. 175–76.

9. Boyd and Yoshida, *Submarine Force,* 126, 134–43, 146–47, 150–57.

10. Boyd and Yoshida, *Submarine Force,* 167–75; O'Neill, *Suicide Squads,* 186–216.

11. Boyd and Yoshida, *Submarine Force,* xiii, appendix 9, "Summary of Submarine Losses in World War II and the Surviving Submarines," 208–17.

12. Calculated from appendix 9, above. There are other lists but all depend for most of their information on the JANAC, *Japanese Naval and Merchant Shipping Losses During World War II By All Causes* (Washington, DC: Navy Department, 1947). Slightly different numbers given in appendix C, "Details of Japanese Submarine Losses," in Hashimoto, *Sunk*, 261–73.

13. Boyd and Yoshida, *Submarine Force*, xiii; Hashimoto, *Sunk*, 164–75.

14. Multiple references on this issue in Boyd and Yoshida, *Submarine Force*, xi–xii, 1–8, 15, 34–35, 49–52, 55, 86–87, 91, 116, 135, 147–48, 158, 175, 188–90. The 1934 instructions are in appendix 1, 191–93; Hashimoto, *Sunk*, 6, 62, 239–40.

15. Charles A. Lockwood, *Sink 'Em All: Submarine Warfare in the Pacific* (New York: E. P. Dutton & Co., 1951), 240.

16. Boyd and Yoshida, *Submarine Force*, 189–90.

17. Hashimoto, *Sunk*, 239.

18. Boyd and Yoshida, *Submarine Force*, 193.

19. Lockwood, *Sink*, counts two losses to Japanese submarines. U.S. losses from Navy History Division, *United States Submarine Losses, World War II* (Washington, DC: U.S.G.P.O., 5th printing, 1963) and Milton, *Subs Against the Rising Sun.*

6

A Fleet in Being

If, on the very eve of the Pacific war, the Japanese Navy had held a grand review of its main battle units, it would have showcased the Imperial Fleet at its historically highest strength. Two decades of massive investment, new construction, extensive retrofitting, and constant, tough, realistic training had produced a world-class navy of impressive potential capability. Three long columns of warships, pennants streaming, could have steamed smartly past the reviewing stand under the observing gaze of the emperor himself. In the central column would steam ten battleships and eighteen heavy cruisers collectively capable of delivering in a very short time broadsides of several thousand tons of steel and high explosive shells on targets many miles away. Included in the column would be the Yamato, the largest and heaviest battleship in the world, armed with 18.1 inch guns, 16 inches of belt and 8 of gun casement armor, capable of speeds up to 27 knots, the tyrannosaurus rex of the world's capital ships. Gliding by in the parallel starboard column would be the light cruisers and destroyer squadrons, much more lightly armed and armored, but swifter and equipped with multiple torpedo launchers whose oxygen powered tubes running at 49 knots were fully capable of sinking enemy ships at distances up to twenty-two thousand yards away. The port column would have included more than sixty state of the art submarines, the Sixth Fleet described in the previous chapter, with cruising ranges up to twelve thousand miles and a collective arsenal of several hundred of their own long-range torpedoes. Behind and bringing up the same column would sail six heavy and four light aircraft carriers with their distinctive flight decks packed with several hundred torpedo planes, dive bombers, interceptors, and patrol aircraft, capable of devastating air strikes—as the Americans were soon to experience—on targets hundreds of miles away. Hundreds of bombers and other warplanes belonging to the land-based naval air fleets would have droned overhead, piloted, as were the carrier planes, by the most rigorously selected and experienced naval aviators in the world. Unseen, but supporting the fleet were hundreds of auxiliary vessels like transports, cargo ships, oilers, sub tenders, repair ships, and patrol boats. Behind the ship crews themselves stood tens of thousands of mechanics, steam fitters, base troops, signal personnel, naval infantry, and the massive apparatus of Japanese ports, naval bases, and shipyards on which an armada of this type depended for maintenance, overhauls, and replenishment.[1]

Great fleets do not appear out of nowhere. This one was the combined and cumulative product of several revolutions: the Meji Restoration, the Industrial Revolution, the all big-gun steel-clad dreadnought, the invention and perfection of submarines and airplanes, aggressive and expansionist nationalism and imperialism, Japan's determination since the First World War to achieve naval parity with Great Britain and America, and the rise of an alliance of fascist powers individually and collectively determined to change radically the world's geopolitical status quo. A review of this fleet, then, would have been an unabashed and spectacular celebration of national pride and identity, imperial polity, armed might, technical modernity, *Realpolitik* possibility, great power status, and Asian racial strength and promise. It is therefore easy to understand, historically, the pride and sense of empowerment and satisfaction that would have been felt by Emperor Hirohito and his subjects at such a review as the sleek predatory shapes steamed by, rising sun flags contrasting with the dark somber sea, a reified symbol of lethal power and potentially unrestrained violence.

But, of course, this review never actually happened in exactly the same manner that we have tried to imagine it. On the very eve of war, there was no time to concentrate the entire strength of the imperial navy at a single location, even if that had been physically possible. For on December 7–8, 1941, this great fleet, subdivided into its various task forces, stood instead off Pearl Harbor, Malaya, and the Philippines, ready to launch the air, naval, and amphibious attacks that, allied to the efforts of Japanese land forces, would sweep the white colonial powers from Pacific Asia, creating in the process a greatly expanded and finally resource self-sufficient Japanese empire.[2]

The Japanese fleet that began the Pacific war shared in common with all the other great navies of the world a distinct strategic and intellectual legacy. The theoretical underpinnings of this legacy were provided by the American navalist Admiral Alfred Thayer Mahan, professor at the U.S. Naval War College and the most influential military thinker on naval warfare in the nineteenth century. In *The Influence of Sea Power on History*, first published in 1890, Mahan argued that great national wealth and power had always in the past been synonymous with control of the seas. Sea power, in its turn, rested on an oceangoing fleet prepared and strong enough to engage and destroy any enemy fleet that challenged it in a decisive sea battle, such as Trafalgar. Published in many editions and translated into many languages, Mahan's work became required reading at naval academies all over the world. And in the highly competitive and militaristic atmosphere of the prewar period, Mahan's general point that national greatness was linked to great navies was avidly seized upon by political leaders, admiralties, and popular naval leagues as ammunition in the military budget battles of the time.[3] It was, for example, in response to Mahanian precepts that Theodore Roosevelt pushed for construction of the Great White Fleet, and that Kaiser Wilhelm II and Admiral Tirpitz challenged British naval supremacy by developing Germany's own great fleet to raise the Reich from great power to world power status.

But exactly how the rapid technical improvements to predreadnought warships would actually fit into Mahan's schema was not at first very clear. Over the long and relatively peaceful nineteenth century, few great sea battles had been fought between the ironclad, steam-powered, screw-propelled, oceangoing battleships armed with breech-loading rifled guns that had eclipsed the wind-driven wooden ships of the line of Nelson's day. How true Mahan's general theory was—that great fleets existed to crush the enemy in a decisive battle—remained undemonstrated. Here the Japanese Navy's destruction of the Russian Fleet at Tsushima in 1905, as historian Ronald Spector notes, served to confirm the fact that despite the great technical changes in warships, the ironclad present would continue to be decided by twentieth century Trafalgars dominated by heavily gunned warships.[4]

But no sooner than Tsushima seemed to repeat history, naval technology again took another great leap forward. Under the influence of First Lord Fisher, Britain introduced the dreadnought—the heavily armored, but speedy, all big-gun ship of enormous displacement—that made the rest of the world's battle fleets obsolete overnight while promising results of a decisiveness and one-sidedness far greater than had ever before been imagined. A new naval competition began as all the great powers raced to lay down their own dreadnought fleets in preparation for the coming decisive battle.[5]

Though the introduction of the dreadnought had evened the playing field by also condemning most of the British Navy to obsolescence, Germany, caught up in the Mahanian dream, but realizing that it would be impossible in the short term to outproduce Britain in this new naval race, sought to justify its much smaller fleet's utility by emphasizing its own distinctive naval strategy based on *Risikogedanke*, or risk theory. The German fleet, conceived of as a *Riskflotte*, would be strong enough so that in a war with Great Britain, it could inflict such losses that the British would lose their numerical superiority over other potential enemies. Even in a position of naval inferiority, then, Germany could achieve her goal by promising the British that the annihilation of Germany's battle fleet would be a Pyrrhic victory.[6]

A less bloodthirsty and slightly paradoxical variation of this strategy was the concept of a "fleet in being," that is, a weaker fleet that survived by avoiding battle, and in doing so continued to pose a constant threat to a superior fleet, tying it down and limiting its strategic capabilities. But of course the problem for Germany in the First World War was that a pure "fleet in being" posed little threat to the British naval blockade that was slowly strangling the German wartime economy. So the Germans hoped to cut the numerical odds by winning smaller battles against parts of the British fleet in separate actions. At Jutland, in 1916, the Germans turned out to be unwilling to risk their *Riskflotte* in a general action. Though indecisive, Jutland nevertheless did demonstrate the enormously destructive powers of dreadnought technology and reaffirmed for naval establishments all over the world the potential for decisive naval battles.[7]

In the postwar period, two younger powers—Japan and the United States—took the lead in laying the foundations for a thoroughly modern world-class fleet of super powerful dreadnoughts supported by submarines, naval aviation, and a new kind of capital ship, the aircraft carrier. By limiting the number and size of traditional types of capital ships, the 1921 Washington Naval Conference and its successor conferences in London actually accelerated this process by providing incentives to pack more powerful armaments into retrofitted or newly constructed warships, to convert capital ships or hulls into aircraft carriers, and to develop fleet air and submarine forces. In this evolution, carrier planes were initially envisioned for reconnaissance rather than a combat role. But experiments soon established that airplanes could sink capital ships with bombs, and within both the Japanese and American navies, a struggle began between the battleship and the carrier admirals, the latter proponents of a more aggressive and ambitious use of fleet air power. On the eve of war, dominant leaders like Yamamoto, King, and Nimitz had emerged to substantially influence the adoption of new organizations, like the fleet carrier group, and new tactics, like the air strike against opposing forces across hundreds of miles of ocean. If the means were evolving, however, the goal of naval warfare remained the same in both navies. Both carrier and battleship admirals remained wedded to the idea of Mahanian decisive battle, as reflected in war plan after war plan. Both emerging naval powers also saw the other as their principal potential maritime enemy, a fact also reflected in their war plans.[8]

The naval agreements, which permanently limited the Japanese fleet to a smaller size than those of the United States or Great Britain, aroused tremendous resentment in Japan. As soon as the militarists seized control of the government in the early 1930s, they greatly increased military spending. At the beginning of 1936, the Japanese government publicly renounced the naval agreements and by 1937 had begun a rapid expansion of the navy including the construction in great secrecy of the Yamato class of super battleships. At roughly the same time, beginning in 1933–1934, the Americans, who had not previously built up to the treaty limits, initiated under President Roosevelt's leadership an ambitious plan, subsequently confirmed and extended, to replace old and build new warships. Nevertheless, the American fleet would not reach the size allowed by the revised treaty limits until 1944.

As a result of all these developments, the Japanese Navy had by the time of Pearl Harbor gained a slight numerical edge in the Pacific over the Americans, who had already committed much of their fleet to the battle for the Atlantic. The losses inflicted on the American fleet, the Royal Navy, and the hastily organized ABCD (America-Britain-China-Netherlands) squadrons at Pearl Harbor and in the Philippines, East Indies, and the Indian Ocean, combined with very light Japanese losses, temporarily increased this margin of superiority. It was, however, not just Japan's ability to concentrate her superior naval forces against scattered and unprepared enemy squadrons that impressed her adversaries. The synergy of excellent ships, superbly trained crews, aggressive leadership, and integrated use of air power enabled the Imperial Navy to outthink, outmaneuver, and outfight the Allied naval contingents decisively despite their desperate resistance. Mahan would have approved.

Yet, as we know, this decisive result turned out to be surprisingly shortlived. The Americans quickly adopted a kind of *Riskflotte* posture, selectively committing their remaining and still potent carrier forces to wear down Japanese forces. This, joined to Combined Fleet's reckless search for a decisive fleet action, led to naval bloodbaths at Midway and in the Solomons. As potent as they were, carriers on both sides also turned out to be terribly vulnerable to air attack from land or other carrier-based planes. By the end of 1942, both sides had lost practically all their carriers. The result was that no carrier-to-carrier battles took place during the following year. In the Solomons there were numerous nighttime ship-to-ship engagements in which Japanese training, at least at first, won victory after victory over Allied naval squadrons. The Solomons and New Guinea campaigns also demonstrated that ships operating within range of land-based planes in daylight without adequate air escort risked almost certain destruction. Japanese determination to regain Guadalcanal and hold advanced positions in New Guinea led to crippling losses of ships, naval planes, and pilots. American *Riskflotte* tactics, combined with increasing land-based air power, inflicted the equivalent of a decisive defeat on the Imperial Navy between mid-1942 and mid-1943.[9]

The American *Riskflotte* strategy also entailed extremely high U.S. losses during this period. But behind the American willingness to play the *Riskflotte* game was the fact that (in a manner that Mahan would have appreciated) anything close to an even exchange was acceptable because America was busy building an overwhelmingly superior *Grossweltmachtflotte* that would first begin coming into action in late 1943. The United States in effect had two Pacific fleets. The first was largely destroyed, out of action, or worn out by the end of 1943, at which time the second took over the task of destroying the remnants of the imperial fleet and completing the defeat of Japan in the Pacific.[10]

The Japanese, on the other hand, had to fight the war with only one fleet, and once that fleet was destroyed, given the limitations of the Japanese industrial base, there was nothing to replace it. The growing numerical disparity that had so clearly begun to manifest itself after two years of war is often cited as proof of the inevitability of ultimate Allied victory and Japanese defeat in the Pacific War. By October 1945 the United States had built and commissioned 141 carriers, 8 battleships, 47 cruisers, and close to one thousand destroyers, escorts, and submarines. By contrast, during the period from the outbreak of war to mid-August 1945, the Japanese produced only 15 aircraft carriers, 1 battleship, 9 cruisers, and slightly more than two hundred destroyers and submarines.[11] While these production truths certainly helped to determine Japan's deteriorating and finally fatal naval situation, they do not constitute irrefutable proof that the historical result of the naval war had to have been decided as early as late 1943 and in exactly the manner that it was in the Pacific. Many of the Japanese Navy's wounds were self-inflicted, and the growing gap between Japanese and American naval capability need not have developed as quickly or as overwhelmingly as it did. A different strategy, along the defense-in-depth lines we have been stressing, would have helped to preserve a Japanese fleet in being for a much longer time while simultaneously preparing for a *Riskflotte* commitment when the opportunity for a decisive naval battle at a key juncture of the war presented itself that would have inflicted enough damage on the Americans to have slowed down, or even brought to a halt, their assaults on key positions on the way to the homeland, even if it meant sacrificing the Japanese fleet.

The Japanese Navy did relentlessly pursue a decisive battle strategy from the beginning of the war until it had no more ships left to fight with. The problem was that, with the exception of Pearl Harbor, the battles it sought and fought all turned out to be decisive Japanese defeats: Midway, the Solomons, the Philippine Sea, and Leyte Gulf. Midway crippled the carrier arm; the Solomons caused critical and irreplaceable losses in the destroyer and submarine arms as well as carrier and land-based naval pilot groups; the Philippine Sea completed the destruction of Japan's carrier force and its air groups; and Leyte Gulf destroyed the remaining and still substantial surface fleet. Growing skill and material and technical superiority, of course, played crucial roles in American victories. Close examination of these defeats, however, reveals certain underlying commonalities that suggest that a different and more favorable outcome was not at the time, as well as in retrospect, beyond the realm of possibility.

For example, one of the principles of Mahanian strategy was concentration of strength for the decisive blow. At none of these defeats was the full might of the Combined Fleet ever deployed. A crucial part of the carrier arm was missing at Midway and a substantial force diverted to the Aleutians, while the powerful supporting surface units operated so far away from the carriers that they were unable to join the battle or even contribute their own antiaircraft and reconnaissance assets to the operation. During the Solomons campaign the fleet was committed in packets and in an uncoordinated way over several critical weeks and months. Despite the movement of Combined Fleet headquarters to Truk in order to direct the Solomons campaign, the full power of its surface and air units was never committed at any one time. Instead, air units and naval divisions were expended in piecemeal attacks that the initially weak Allies were able to match, while destroyer and submarines suffered high losses in misconceived supply and reinforcement missions. Both Midway and the Solomons were the result of overexpansion and overcommitment of forces too far from supporting bases and within range of enemy land-based air. Both the Philippine Sea and Leyte Gulf repeated this lack of coordination, the former fought almost entirely alone by the carrier force with inadequately trained and inexperienced pilots, the latter involved only units of the surface fleet, and in both cases adequate land-based air support never materialized. And while neither represented strategic overextension—they were instead intended as decisive counterattacks—they ended up being fought on the enemy's terms and against great odds.

How could these outcomes have been different? In thinking through alternate possibilities, the first thing to note is how close the Japanese Navy came to success on some of these occasions. As much as Midway was a misconceived adventure, almost all students of the battle stress the role that pure chance played in the loss of four Japanese fleet carriers and the survival of two of the three U.S. carriers. The Japanese attack groups had plenty enough force to have taken Midway, and if closed up to the carriers could have done so simultaneously. The proper criticism of Japan's Midway is that in his strategic search for a decisive battle, Yamamoto put together an unnecessary and overcomplicated plan that risked much and that even if successful, gained a forward position that could not have been held. At Guadalcanal the Japanese Navy had an early opportunity to inflict heavy, perhaps unsupportable, losses on the cargo and troop ships of the American invasion force, but, content with a tactical victory over Allied warships and overly concerned about its own safety, turned back. If the entire Combined Fleet, surface and air units, had pounced on Guadalcanal and, despite losses, stayed in those waters and relentlessly destroyed Allied transports and supply ships *along with* warships, it might have forced a quasi-permanent American retreat. Failure of the Allied effort on Guadalcanal could have had a tremendous effect on the Allies' counterattack and demonstrated the futility of committing substantial American forces to the Pacific.

But the Japanese fleet never made that effort. Despite the fierce air and sea battles around Guadalcanal, the Japanese in the Solomons fought the wrong battle at the wrong time and in the wrong way. The battle of Leyte Gulf, that decisive coup de grace to the Japanese Navy, also represented a lost opportunity. For one of the few times in the war, powerful Japanese surface units, including a Yamato class battleship, came within gunnery range of a temporarily unprotected invasion fleet of hundreds of supply and transport vessels. But Admiral Ozawa lost his nerve and turned back in the face of bluffing by a few American destroyers and escort carriers. And to what purpose? Preservation of his units took precedence over delivery of an extremely damaging blow, which might have significantly delayed American plans for reconquest of the Philippines, along with Saipan the key position in defense of the homeland.

At no time did the Japanese Navy strike with its fully concentrated force. At no time did the Japanese Navy strike in a manner that effectively combined its air and surface units or push on to decisive results when they were within reach (even Pearl Harbor might be mentioned here). When decisive results or at least the possibility of inflicting severe losses on a significant part of the U.S. fleet was operationally in reach, Japanese naval commanders inexplicably lacked the will to relentlessly pursue a temporarily vulnerable enemy, and withdrew. No Horatio Nelson emerged, prepared even if it meant sacrificing his force to inflict enough damage to have limited American strategic options and delayed penetration of Japan's defense-in-depth zone. In Mahanian terms, then, the Japanese frittered away a significant part of their navy in ill-chosen actions during the first two years of war, thereby compromising its utility as a fleet in being, while also failing to operate as a *Riskflotte* by striking a single massive concentrated blow against a significant portion of the U.S. fleet. This collective failure did not go unnoticed among the high command. Admiral Ugaki's invaluable war diary, for example, is full of ruminations and descriptions of staff debates over the proper operational role the navy should play in order to defeat or at least to stop the Americans.[12]

The Japanese Navy could not and probably would never have been able ultimately to withstand the finally overwhelming numbers and technical skills of the fully developed U.S. Navy. As one recent historian points out, the American fleet that inflicted the final defeat on Japan was overwhelmingly composed of ships that were either commissioned or constructed after Pearl Harbor.[13] While wearing the Japanese down did indeed entail their own high losses, the Americans were simultaneously constructing the brand new, numerically and technically superior fleet that rapidly finished off the Japanese Navy during 1944.

Yet as we have argued throughout this book, the real alternative to overwhelming defeat for Japan lay not in some corresponding overwhelming Japanese victory, but in avoiding overexpansion, building an integrated in-depth imperial defense, refusing to play the attrition game, fighting more effectively, and surviving longer, forcing the Americans to realize that their goal of an absolutely overwhelming total victory over Japan would not be worth its cost. Faced with a less one-sided and longer war, one that delayed the approach to Japan proper into 1946 or 1947, American war weariness, the enormous pressure to reduce the financial burden of war, the fallout with the Allies, and the danger of a permanently destabilized or communist postwar Asia might have forced the Americans to conclude that the cost of total defeat of Japan had come to outweigh the benefits.

What was the most important contribution the Japanese Navy could have made to this end? We have already identified two general—the avoidance of overextension and construction of a defense in-depth—and two specific areas—convoys and escorts, and a commerce-raiding submarine campaign—that were within the capability of the navy if a different course had been set. The ideas for all were there, but they were either never adopted or implemented too late.

Despite its nautical dimensions, the defense of the empire could not, of course, depend on the Japanese Navy alone. For one thing, land-based airplanes flying from multiple hardened airfields were capable of contesting enemy vessels and aircraft operating within their range. This is, after all, why the occupation of key points and construction of airfields so obsessed both sides and were the ultimate objectives of almost all naval and amphibious operations in the Pacific. And though carrier forces could be quite useful in providing offensive airpower beyond the range of land-based planes, they were quite vulnerable to enemy air attacks when forced to sacrifice their mobility in order to provide close support of land operations over any extended period of time. Their proper role was the destruction of the opposing fleet and the protection of their own. Furthermore, the construction and manning of static land defenses was not a fleet mission, even if naval personnel and air assets were integrated into the defenses of key points on land. It took infantry forces, hardened defenses, and artillery fire to fight enemy infantry forces trying to come ashore or once they had gained a foothold. This was more properly the realm of the Japanese Army, which, as we will see, could have been much more effectively employed in defending the Pacific approaches to the homeland. Recall that Prime Minister Tojo laid responsibility for Japan's defeat directly at the feet of the Imperial Navy in two areas: its inability to prevent the raids of U.S. carrier forces or to stop the American amphibious forces from leapfrogging Japanese land defenses. These were the proper objects of fleet action.

In analyzing the possibility of a more successful role for the Japanese Navy than the historical case, it is important first of all to understand American limitations and vulnerabilities. After all, the imbalance of power that developed between American and Japanese fleets was a somewhat late development. As mentioned, Japanese naval forces enjoyed a slight numerical edge at the onset of war, an edge that actually increased due to slight losses and heavy Allied losses during the first six months of the war. It was not until well into 1944 that American multiple carrier task forces and huge, heavily gunned invasion support groups began their deep penetration of the empire. The fact was that U.S. resources in the Pacific were finite and that American forces operated under serious logistical and facility limits. For example, the immense number of American-produced warships is often compared to the small number of new fleet units produced by the Japanese Navy during the war, as if this simple juxtaposition constitutes sufficient explanation of the defeat of the Japanese Navy. What is usually overlooked is that many American ships were constructed too late to take part in the war. Though they would have come on station later, the United States was never actually able to get an important portion of its warship construction into action before August 1945. Also, throughout most of the war a significant portion of all American warship production had to be dedicated to the battle for the Atlantic and amphibious operations in the Mediterranean and European theaters. Perhaps most important, from beginning to end there were drastic shortages of transport and cargo vessels in the Pacific, shortages exacerbated by the enormous distances involved and the need to construct port and freight-handling facilities from scratch. The only great Asian port that fell to the Allies throughout the war was Manila, where Japanese resistance was not finally overcome until March 1945. Shipping constraints bedeviled U.S. strategic decisions throughout the war and even forced the postponement or cancellation of projected operations like the invasion of Formosa or landings on the Chinese coast. There was a limit to the number of troops, planes, and warships that could operate and be supported in the Pacific theater that fell far short of the total resources available to the Allies. The United States found it very difficult, if not impossible, to mount more than one major operation at a time on the scale of Leyte, Luzon, or Okinawa. Even at the end of the war, with Japan almost completely prostrate, the invasion of the Home Islands had to be broken into two major landings separated by a time lapse of many months. Nor did the end of the war in Europe in May 1945 completely break this logjam because the rapid repatriation (under tremendous public pressure) of U.S. troops from Europe and the need for enormous immediate postwar civilian aid to Europe continued to tie down mercantile assets. By August 1945, the United States was already rapidly drawing down its war effort while at the same time preparing for the invasion of Japan. How politically acceptable would it have been to postpone the wind-down of U.S. forces if the Japanese had managed to postpone the progress of American forces in the Pacific by months or even years? As Richard Frank's *Downfall* makes clear, against all odds the Japanese had managed to build up defense forces on the southern home island of Kyushu that were substantial enough to cause Admirals King and Nimitz to prepare to withdraw their support from Operation Olympic, the projected November invasion of Japan.[14] In other words, even the enormous military superiority enjoyed by the United States in mid-1945 did not guarantee a conventional military decision over Japan within some acceptable level of casualties. In the end it was the use of atomic weapons that ended the war and made the invasion of Japan moot. But the deployment and use of the atomic bomb was itself dependent upon a long string of military contingencies that had brought them in range only after Japan's urban areas had already largely been erased through conventional strategic bombing operations.

The imperial fleet could have made a much more important contribution to a successful delay of the American advance on the Home Islands. But the Combined Fleet should *not* have been used to fight the American Navy as it did early in the war. It should instead have been saved as a reserve force, a fleet in being, as long as possible, and then committed in a *Riskflotte* operation at a key juncture, striking a decisive blow even if it involved its sacrifice. We have stressed the basic mistakes of overexpansion and being drawn into an attritional game on American terms early in the war. The reason this is so important is not only the fact of avoiding the losses incurred at Midway or in the South Pacific. It is that the Japanese Navy was geometrically less effective when deployed in packets. Its strength as a great fleet derived from the coordinated working together of all its constituent parts. The basic principle of concentration of force is salient here. Before the advent of tactical nuclear weapons, tactical concentration of warships, both dreadnoughts and carriers, as the Americans quickly learned, was an essential feature of providing effective massed antiaircraft fire. An intact Japanese fleet would have had enough capital ships and other combat assets to make it a very formidable and dangerous foe when concentrated. When committed piecemeal, its destructive and defensive capacity was much reduced. The Americans understood this full well. Despite the strategic daring shown during their advance, American admirals were actually quite cautious about committing capital ship task forces at any time or place where they were unable to account for the whereabouts of the Combined Fleet's major components. It was only after the battles of the Philippine Sea and Leyte Gulf in

1944 that they could afford to relax their fears about a Japanese fleet in being. In other words, as long as the battle fleet continued to survive as a potential threat, the more cautious the U.S. Navy had to be.

Objections could, of course, be raised about this line of reasoning. One
is that the United States and its allies had broken Japanese military and
diplomatic codes and in combination with other types of intelligence, were
largely able to estimate Japanese fleet strength and track its movements.
John Prados' *Combined Fleet Decoded* clearly shows how code breaking and
intelligence work provided the Americans with many knowledge advantages. But the reading of codes did not always make Japanese intentions
transparent. Both the Philippine Sea and Leyte Gulf—the two battles that
completed the destruction of the Combined Fleet—started with strategic
surprise on the side of the Japanese. In the former, combined land-based
and carrier aircraft launched at long range initially stole a march on U.S.
forces operating in the Marianas. It was lack of execution and pilot experience rather than Japan's lack of ability to get their navy within range of
American forces that decided the battle. Leyte Gulf was an even more striking example of the possibility of achieving enough surprise. A stealthy
nighttime course reversal and American errors enabled powerful Japanese
surface units to move into position to wreck havoc on the American transport and supply ships crowding the Leyte anchorage. It was lack of execution again—the refusal of Ozawa to press home his attack—that saved the
American invasion fleet from a severe and perhaps debilitating beating. The
point is that the Japanese Navy, even after taking the numerical and technical superiority of the Americans into account, maintained the ability until
fairly late in the war to move formidable naval forces against American
naval concentrations across great distances and with some chance of strategic surprise. How different would it have been if the Combined Fleet had
somehow managed to be at near full strength in mid- to late 1944.

Objection may also be made to the notion of withholding the fleet from
action. What shape would Japanese defenses have been in if portions of the
fleet had not been thrown into the early peripheral actions that did, after
all, inflict heavy losses on the Allies? How far and how quickly could the
Americans have advanced in the absence of fleet opposition? This is a fair
question, and one that obviously influenced Japanese thinking at the time.

To a great extent, the answer to this question depends on an appreciation
of the unique problems of fighting a war in the south and southwestern Pacific. Until late 1943 the brunt of the Allied counterattack fell on the
Solomons and New Guinea. Even if small in scale compared to other theaters, the fighting there was ferocious and deadly for both sides. But the
chief limiting factor was logistics. Lack of shipping, and in MacArthur's area,
inadequate naval force, made distance and nature the principal obstacles
that the Allies had to overcome. From beginning to end, the pace of the Al-

lied counteroffensive against Rabaul was dictated more by the lack of working ports and loading/unloading facilities than the intensity of the fighting itself. Given the material and logistical limitations that would have to have been overcome in any case, we can doubt that the Allied advance up the Solomons and the northern coast of New Guinea could have been accelerated very much even in the absence of strong Japanese resistance. Fleet and carrier-type operations in the surrounding waters were difficult and dangerous. Moving in daylight without adequate land-based air cover was very risky for supply and transport ships. The fighting on land was conducted in the most environmentally hostile and debilitating theater in the entire war. Nor, on the Japanese side, should operations there have been a priority. Far more important would have been construction and completion of the defense zone far deeper in the empire, which meant great investment in infrastructure, construction of hardened and mutually supportive airfields, and establishing reliable routes of supply beyond the strategic reach of the enemy.

A far more important fleet mission in that situation and at that stage of the war would have been to conserve its strength, enlarge and train its carrier groups, and to function as a potent fleet-in-being threat within the framework of a deep defense-in-depth zone. The goal would not have been to avoid combat forever but to maximize nonnaval defense resources, cut needless losses by refusing to waste the fleet on minor objectives, and avoid combat on American terms.

Ultimately American strategic choices in the Pacific were few and stark. To advance close enough to the Home Islands to launch an effective strategic bombing campaign or to stage a successful amphibious invasion of Japan itself, the Americans had to seize one or all of the three strategic objectives that the geography of the approaches into the empire dictated: the Marianas, the Philippines, or Formosa. Those places were the keys to ultimate victory over Japan. To confront the United States with longer and more effective resistance, they had to be defended more successfully than in the historical case. We will have more to say about the project of successfully defending these areas, but the fact that the Americans had to take them sooner or later and could only do so with naval and amphibious forces inevitably would present Japanese forces, and particularly the navy, with opportunities to derail the American advance.

Though Formosa was eventually dropped from the list by the Americans, the invasions of the Marianas and the Philippines, like the subsequent stormings of Iwo Jima and Okinawa, were gigantic military and naval operations. They required the U.S. Navy to concentrate its strength in a fairly limited area for a substantial length of time, both during the landings and in subsequent fighting until a successful lodgment had been achieved and airfields built. These concentrations of warships, transports, cargo vessels, and landing ships and craft represented a huge and vulnerable sitting target. It was exactly their massive naval appurtenances that should have been the target of the entire strength of the preserved Japanese fleet in being.

How different it would have been if Combined Fleet had somehow managed to be at near full strength in mid- to late 1944. A Japanese fleet whose strength had not been frittered away would have possessed a very much larger carrier force than in the historical case, extremely powerful heavy surface units and adequate numbers of light cruisers and destroyers. In some technical areas, such as radar and intelligence, it would have been eclipsed by the Americans. But it would not have been ground down by protracted attritional operations. It would instead have been ready to be deployed when inevitably, a rare, but real, opportunity came to strike a decisive blow on American forces tied down in a major offensive against an unavoidable target. Among those, Saipan was probably the most important because successful resistance there would have pushed back the date that was the soonest the Americans managed, historically, to begin the aerial destruction of urban Japan by massive firebombing. Successful resistance at Saipan also could only have been interpreted as a clear sign that Japan was capable of defending its inner empire and that her defeat was neither near nor certain.

But how rational would it have been to bet the empire and the entire battle fleet on such a naval ride of the Valkeryies? The problem is that in thinking through the alternatives, it is impossible to imagine a more disastrous end than what actually happened to the Japanese Navy historically. Such a *Riskflotte* operation would at least have had the potential to transform the Pacific War into a much more problematic proposition than it already was for the Americans by inflicting unacceptable losses in one blow and knocking the props out from under their delicately balanced offensive schedule. Japanese admirals had always sought, and properly so, to inflict a decisive naval defeat on the Americans. But they had initially sought decisiveness at the wrong time and place, and subsequently at the right places but with greatly reduced strength and in a compromised imperial defense system that, done differently, would have multiplied the fleet's deadliness and provided it with the proper strategic opportunities.

NOTES

1. There are many sources for the Japanese Navy's order of battle and the technical specifications of her ships. Besides the sources on submarines noted in the previous chapter, I have relied primarily on Jentschura, Jung, and Mickel, *Warships of the Imperial Japanese Navy, 1869–1945*; Dull, *Battle History*; and the appendices to Fleet Admiral Ernest J. King's three *Official Reports to the Secretary of the Navy*, published, along with the Official Reports of Marshall and Arnold, in *The War Reports of . . .*

Marshall . . . Arnold . . . King (Philadelphia: J. B. Lippincott & Co., 1944–45), 724–78, esp. 724–38.

2. For fleet and task force compositions throughout the war, Dull, *Battle History;* and the many volumes of Morison's *HUSNO.*

3. For a succinct portrayal of Mahan's influence, Robert L. O'Connell, *Sacred Vessels: The Cult of the Battleship and the Rise of the U.S. Navy* (New York: Oxford University Press, 1991), 60–71, 93–100. *Sacred Vessels* is a veritable history of modern battle fleet theory and practice by all the great powers. Also Spector, *At War At Sea,* 1–25; and John Keegan, *The Price of Admiralty: The Evolution of Naval Warfare* (New York: Viking, 1989).

4. Spector, *At War At Sea,* 24.

5. Keegan, *The Price of Admiralty,* 97–106; Spector, *At War At Sea,* 22–29; O'Connell, *Sacred Vessels,* 101–26.

6. O'Connell, *Sacred Vessels,* 116–17; Keegan, *The Price of Admiralty,* 100–103; Keith Yates, *Flawed Victory: Jutland 1916* (Annapolis, MD: Naval Institute Press, 2000), 9–13.

7. For the battle of Jutland: Keegan, *The Price of Admiralty,* 97–155; O'Connell, *Sacred Vessels,* 153–90; Spector, *At War At Sea,* 64–102. Yates, *Flawed Victory,* is an excellent recent study.

8. Spector, *At War At Sea,* 122–64.

9. Morison's *HUSNO* volumes, of course, but an excellent narrative of the war at sea during this early period is Spector, *At War At Sea,* 152–55, 185–223, and for the later naval war, 258–59, 275–313; Midway and carrier warfare is well covered by Keegan, *The Price of Admiralty,* 157–211. Dull's *Battle History,* with its heavy use of Japanese records, presents the naval war from the perspective of the imperial navy.

10. Willmott, *The War with Japan,* 158–59.

11. Ellis, *Brute Force,* tables 57–60 in the "Statistical Appendix," 64–66. An enormous number of statistical tables on every conceivable aspect of the war can be found in Ellis, *World War II: The Encyclopedia of Facts and Figures* and Dunnigan and Nofi, *Victory at Sea: World War II in the Pacific.*

12. Ugaki, *Fading Victory,* passim.

13. Willmott, *The War with Japan,* 158–59.

14. Frank, *Downfall,* 147.

7

The Battle for the Skies

They came, usually at twilight, or dawn, solitary intruders, squadrons, waves of hundreds, to smash their planes, their explosives, and themselves against American shipping and naval forces in and around the island of Okinawa. Slipping, sliding, weaving, gliding, they bore in from every possible angle and compass point. Most approached in a controlled dive from high altitude then dropped vertically at high speed onto their targets. Some skimmed the ocean surface in horizontal attacks against the sides of ships. Others approached at low level, went into a steep climb, rolled over, and crashed into decks, command bridges, funnels, and guns.

Such organized and deliberate suicide air attacks were not new to the Americans, who had first encountered them, though not in such numbers, in the Philippines. At Okinawa the Americans had carefully prepared their defense against such attacks. Sixty or more miles from the island were stationed radar-equipped destroyers to provide early warning of air attacks. Combat air patrols continually circled over the picket ships and the invasion fleet. In the anchorage itself, radar and computer directed 5-inch guns to fire deadly proximity fuse shells at the attackers. Rapid-fire guns crowding almost every ship deck and superstructure threw up their own wall of close range 20- and 40-millimeter fire. During attacks smog generators covered the invasion force with a low-lying haze to reduce visibility. Radar-guided night fighters searched for enemy planes attempting to approach their targets under the cover of darkness. Far beyond the island and the picket line, carrier planes and B-29 very heavy bombers pounded the airfields on Kyushu and Formosa from which most of the attackers came.

Many of the enemy never reached the target area, falling victim to preemptive raids, mechanical problems, bad weather, navigational errors, and omnipresent American interceptors. Those who somehow managed to reach the anchorage were usually knocked down by the hail of antiaircraft fire put up by every American ship. But the Japanese suicide planes kept coming day after day—some ten major attacks in all—and some always got through. Because their approach was often combined with hundreds of conventional attacks, it was difficult to pick them out until the very last moment—the high-speed approach gave their targets only a minute for visual observation and twenty seconds to fire their close-range guns. No American ship, from the smallest minesweeper to the largest fleet carrier or battleship, was safe from attack. And the damage caused by the impact at high terminal velocity of one or several tons of aircraft, stuffed with bombs, explosives, and aviation fuel, could be devastating. Even a near miss could sink or damage their intended victims.[1]

Altogether, between March and August of 1945, the Japanese flew some two thousand kamikaze and five thousand conventional air sorties against the Americans at Okinawa. The aerial assault scored hits on 346 U.S. ships, sinking thirty-four, and damaging forty-three so badly that they were removed from service or were still undergoing repair at the end of the war. U.S. naval personnel casualties were equally horrific: some 4,900 sailors died and 4,800 were wounded by the aerial onslaught.[2] It was the highest number of casualties of any naval engagement fought during World War II and the bloodiest battle in American naval history. Sailors quickly learned that even if its pilot was killed and an incoming plane was shot to pieces, momentum might still carry it into their ship. Each attack successfully defended was soon followed by others. From the lowest ranker in the engine room to the captain on the ship's bridge, no sailor was safe. The chronic tension and terror caused by the continuous attacks, the growing casualty lists, and the gruesome wounds and deaths inflicted by shipboard fires and explosions also led to an increase in another category of casualty: an alarming 50 percent increase in psychiatric casualties as men went mad, had breakdowns, and succumbed to combat fatigue. The situation was so extreme and physical and mental casualties so heavy that the American authorities for months suppressed the facts for fear of the impact they might have on the public.[3]

The kamikazes, however, were only one element, and a rather late one, in a larger and more complicated Pacific air war. From beginning to end, fighting in the Pacific had been as much or more a struggle for the skies as the seas, and indeed the latter was quite dependent on the former. Since there were no territories, resources, or populations in the south and central Pacific that were intrinsically valuable, the places from which airpower could be projected became the strategic prizes.[4] Campaigns in those areas therefore aimed at taking and holding airfields from which one side's warplanes would attempt to neutralize enemy airfields within their operating radius, thus making the surrounding waters safe for their vessels and dangerous for those of the enemy. Both Japan's initial outward expansion, and the American counteroffensive took the form of a series of strategic hops from one point to the next, with land-based planes and carriers serving as mobile air bases operating against enemy air and naval forces and providing air cover and ground support for the water-borne invading forces whose job it was to seize existing airfields or to secure places where new ones could be constructed.

By late 1943, Japan's air forces had lost this decisive struggle, and throughout 1944 the Allies had accelerated their drives up the New Guinea coast and through the central Pacific, converging at the Philippine Islands. As the power of U.S. Army and Navy air forces grew and Japanese air resistance waned, it became increasingly difficult for the Japanese warplanes to mount any kind of effective air operation against their opponent. To make matters worse, U.S. planes soon joined their submarine force in attacking Japanese shipping, initiated the strategic bombing campaign against the homeland, and undertook aerial mining of imperial waters. As more and more of the ill-prepared and poorly defended interior of the empire became prey to American aircraft, the threads that held the empire together began to unravel at an alarming pace.

Given the ultimately overwhelming nature of American airpower in all its manifestations in the Pacific, it may seem to be tilting at windmills to suggest that even in this area Japan had the capability to fight a much more successful war. In examining the decline of Japanese airpower, however, two stark facts stand out. First, at the beginning of the war Japanese air forces enjoyed significant advantages and quickly established air superiority throughout the Pacific. Second, the ensuing destruction of Japanese airpower was the direct result of her early overextension and acceptance of an attritional struggle against the Americans in the South Pacific during the next two years of war.

Japan began the war with formidable air forces. Her factories produced 5,088 planes of all types in 1941, and the army and navy together went to war with 6,000 planes, including about 2,520 first line planes. The navy alone started the war with 2,210 planes, including about 650 carrier and 500 land-based planes, with the balance consisting principally of float planes of various types.[5] The quality of planes ranged from the capable to outstanding. In the navy's AM6 Zero fighter Japan had perhaps the finest interceptor/escort plane in the world. Fast, very agile, and with outstanding range, in the hands of a good navy pilot it was capable of outfighting any aircraft the Allies sent against it in the first year of the war. Navy pilots also flew a number of serviceable dive bomber and torpedo plane types that wreaked havoc on Allied warships in the early months of the war. Both services also flew adequate types and numbers of long-range land-based light and medium bombers that were capable of highly accurate bombing under the conditions of air superiority the Japanese quickly established in the Pacific. Though many of its squadrons took part in the initial conquests of Malaysia, Indonesia, and Burma, army air formations remained concentrated until 1943 principally in Manchuria, facing the Soviets, or in China, where they faced little aerial opposition. Fighting in the Pacific regions was undertaken primarily by the naval air arm, and it was on its pilots and planes, both carrier and land-based, that the fighting at Midway and in the Solomons fell. The navy's highly selective training program—generally four and a half to five years long—produced the best pilots in the world. Most naval pilots entered the war with at least seven hundred hours of flight time under their belt, and many had also acquired wartime flying experience in support of Japanese forces in China in the 1930s.[6] It was these men who rapidly destroyed the greatly inferior allied air forces in the Pacific in 1941 and early 1942.

Despite their early accomplishments, however, there were structural weaknesses that were to haunt Japan's air forces throughout the war. One was a shortage of pilots. On the eve of the war the naval training program, for example, graduated only some one hundred new pilots a year. Suggestions to expand the training program and build up a pool of fifteen thousand pilots had earlier been rejected. As a result, at the time of Pearl Harbor there were only 1,500 navy pilots for 2,200 first line aircraft. Though the navy did expand the pilot training program, it continued to be constricted in 1942 by the retention of the requirement of seven hundred hours of flying time to qualify for combat, which was finally reduced to five hundred hours in 1943. But the restricted numbers of new pilots produced was not enough to replace the talented veteran pilots and aces that had begun the war. Japan would eventually train a total of about sixty thousand pilots over the course of the war, but from mid-1943 quality plummeted as pilot candidates began receiving increasingly rudimentary flight instruction.[7]

Japanese aircraft also suffered from the fact that their design valued light airframes, range, and agility over sturdiness and survivability. By western standards their engines were underpowered and unreliable, particularly for high altitude operations, and the planes themselves underarmed. Worse still, the lightly constructed models had no armor protection for pilot or crew and no self-sealing fuel tanks. It took very little damage to destroy them. Bombers and slower craft were particularly vulnerable, but even the Zero depended on speed and maneuverability rather than robustness to stay alive.[8]

Another problem was limited production capacity, which even in 1941 was only a fraction of U.S. output. Attempts to increase production did bear fruit. Between 1941 and 1943 combined production of all types more than tripled and then almost doubled again in 1944. For the whole war a respectable total of 76,320 planes were produced. But the bigger production runs were achieved largely by continuing to produce older types. Construction of newer designs, some quite outstanding, faced growing material shortages, particularly in alloys and poorly constructed and tested engines, and were never produced in adequate numbers.[9]

The Americans also entered the war with substantial air forces: 17,600 planes of all types, including 8,500 navy planes that by themselves outnumbered the total available to both Japanese services. But this numerical edge is somewhat misleading. In the all-important category of carrier planes, for example, the Americans could deploy 640, slightly less than the Japanese Navy.[10] After the preemptive strikes on Pearl Harbor and Clark Field in the Philippines, the United States was the inferior in suitable warplanes in the Pacific. This was purely temporary and would soon be reversed by American production. But the provision of new planes to the Pacific was always complicated by the priority given by the president to Lend Lease and by the Army Air Force to the European theater. This meant that for more than a year the Americans in the Pacific fought with inferior or obsolescent aircraft that, initially at least, were outclassed by Japanese machines.

Nevertheless, in the area of airpower the Americans held some great advantages. For one thing the United States did not suffer from the same structural constraints that hindered Japanese airpower. Even before the war the aircraft industry had expanded its annual production of all types of planes, and in 1941 produced five times, and in 1942, six times as many planes as Japan. In 1944 alone the United States would produce some ninety-six thousand planes, more than Japan produced during the entire war.[11] With the exception of navy types, however, in the beginning the great majority of new planes went to Europe. But by the end of the war the United States had roughly half of its immense and modern air fleet in the Pacific.[12]

Although in 1941 the ready American forces in the Pacific consisted largely of obsolescent types, newer and more capable carrier and air force planes were beginning to be introduced and even more advanced designs were on the way. In contrast to the Japanese, the early American types tended to be slower, less maneuverable, and shorter ranged, but had heavier airframes, more reliable engines, armor protected cockpits, self-sealing fuel tanks, and heavier armament. Compared to Japanese planes, they were very rugged, and these technical differences increased in favor of the Americans throughout the war. Even in mid-1942, by adopting tactics that accentuated their strengths, like the ability to operate better at high altitudes, or to dive faster, avoiding the strengths that Japanese aircraft enjoyed, and taking advantage of the vulnerabilities of enemy planes, in the hands of experienced pilots they were quite capable of holding their own in the air war. American bombers were also robust, very heavily armed, possessed great range, and carried good payloads.[13]

Furthermore, the United States entered the war with adequate numbers of pilots. The navy alone had 3,500 regular pilots, more than twice that of its Japanese counterpart, and a pool of 6,000 reservists. The relative inexperience of American front line pilots is often exaggerated. At the beginning of the war half of the regular navy pilots had more than six hundred hours and a quarter more than a thousand, with the remainder having anywhere from three hundred to six hundred hours under their belt, which means that the American Navy could actually deploy just as many experienced pilots as the Japanese Navy. After Pearl Harbor the resources devoted to training increased rapidly. American training took eighteen months, and the minimum number of flight hours required rose from 305 in 1941–1942 to 500 and then 525 hours in 1943–1945. By 1944 the American Navy alone was producing 8,000 new pilots per month. By contrast minimum standards for Japanese pilots declined from 700 hours in 1941–1942 to 500 in 1943, 275 in 1944, and 90 in 1945.[14]

But to read history backward from the depths to which Japanese airpower had fallen in 1944 or 1945 would, of course, be quite teleological. It was not inevitable that the ruin of Japanese airpower in the Pacific take place as rapidly or in exactly the same manner as it unfolded historically. As Dunnigan and Nofi remind us in *Victory at Sea*:

> The Pacific war was the first naval war in which aircraft played a decisive role. Since manned flight was only thirty-eight years old when Pearl Harbor was attacked, there was not a lot of experience in the use of aircraft at war. Aircraft technology had been changing at a breakneck pace through the 1930s; the Japanese attack on Pearl Harbor was, in fact the first massed use of carrier aircraft in combat. Six months later, there was the first carrier-versus-carrier battle. But it was land-based aircraft that truly ruled the skies over the Pacific. Carriers were normally too few in number to cope with land-based airpower. Carriers were used to seize islands that could serve as airfields for the more numerous and capable land-based aircraft. All of this was new to warfare and the air generals and admirals had to write the book as they went along.[15]

It was not only structural, production, or training problems that led to the decline of Japanese airpower in 1942–1943. The defeat grew directly out of mistaken strategic and operational decisions, errors in deploying assets, insistence on reinforcing failure, and the absence of proper integration into deep imperial defenses. As important as the technicalities of the air war were, in other words, it was other factors that determined victory and defeat in the skies in the early part of the war. A different set of decisions and actions, we will argue, would have put Japanese airpower in a much better position to battle the tremendous upsurge in American airpower that began in late 1943.

As Eric Bergerud's fine study of the war in the South Pacific, *Fire in the Sky*, reminds us, the balance of forces in the air was relatively even well into

1943.[16] It is true that the Japanese carrier arm was severely crippled at Midway. But the Americans had also lost most of their carriers by the end of 1942, and for the next year the air war was dominated by land-based aviation. The principal problems facing both sides were the number of operational aircraft available, the provision of bases from which to fly them, and development of support facilities. Even in the Guadalcanal campaign, however, Japanese planes faced far greater difficulties than the Allies did. Though Rabaul quickly became an enormous air and navy base, joining Truk as one of the two main bastions in the Pacific, the lack of airfields on the intermediate islands of the Solomon chain forced Japanese Navy planes, especially fighters, to operate at the very end of their operational range during the struggle for Henderson Field, while unprotected Japanese bombers became the easy prey of American interceptors, who could make multiple sorties each day and spend more time in actual combat in the air. Japanese determination to retake Guadalcanal soon entangled their naval air arm in a grim war of attrition. Trading plane for plane and pilot for pilot was not a winning tactic against an enemy that slowly but surely built up its capacity to replace both at a more rapid rate than the Japanese. American construction techniques, more highly mechanized and vastly more efficient than the handiwork of Japanese labor battalions, also enabled them to construct the needed facilities—runways, taxiways, revetments, and depots—much faster than the Japanese, whose best bases, by American standards, remained quite rudimentary.[17] Nevertheless, it was a continuing nightmare for both sides to fight an air war in the South Pacific. Operating conditions were so bad that a high percentage of all plane losses were due to accidents caused by poor maintenance, primitive runways, weather extremes, and pilot and navigational error. Even the increasingly better supported and equipped Americans suffered from high operational losses.

But rather than pull back from an arena in which they operated at an increasing disadvantage, the Japanese redoubled their efforts to maintain and reinforce their air strength in the Solomons. To sustain the struggle, Combined Fleet had to commit its remaining carrier air groups to operate from land bases in the area, critically undermining efforts to rebuild its carrier forces after the debacle at Midway. At the same time, the progress of the Allies across and around the Owen Stanley Range forced the High Command to feed large army air formations, largely stripped from Manchuria, into the New Guinea theater. Both of these steps merely served to reinforce failure in the South Pacific at the price of stripping the central Pacific of planes, aircrews, and other resources needed to hold off American carriers and invading forces in late 1943 and 1944.

The extent to which the South Pacific became the graveyard of Japanese naval airpower is illustrated by statistics on Japanese naval aircraft losses compiled by Commander J. Fukamizu after the war, summarized in table 7.1.

Table 7.1. Plane Losses of the Japanese Navy Air Force, 1942–1944

Type	FY 1942–1943					FY 1943–1944					Overall Total
	Combat	%	Operational	%	Total	Combat	%	Operational	%	Total	
Fighter	822	52	768	48	1,590	1,170	41	1,673	59	2,843	4,433
Tactical Bombers	631	83	131	17	762	367	31	824	69	1,191	1,953
Medium Bomber	291	63	174	37	465	306	32	663	68	969	1,434
Totals	1,744	61	1,073	38	2,817	1,843	37	3,160	63	5,003	7,820

With the exception of Midway, almost all the naval air losses incurred during this period were in the South Pacific. In the 1942–1943 fiscal year, losses amounted to 2,817 planes and almost doubled to 5,003 planes in 1943–1944, a total of 7,820 planes over the entire two years. To put this in perspective, about 800 Japanese Army Air Force planes were lost in New Guinea, and the U.S. Navy, Marine Corps, and Army Air Force combined lost about 2,000 planes in the South Pacific from all causes in the same period.[18]

Besides illustrating cumulative navy plane losses, table 7.1 also reflects an increasing percentage of operational as opposed to combat losses over time: from 38 percent of all losses in the first year to 63 percent in the second. So while operational losses almost tripled, actual combat losses increased only slightly even though the Americans established an overall favorable kill ratio in combat of 3 to 1.[19] This tells us that as the condition of repeatedly bombed airfields worsened, supporting infrastructure deteriorated or was destroyed, and as the original group of highly skilled pilots were lost and replaced by more inexperienced and poorly trained pilots, the Japanese Navy Air Force (JNAF) found it increasingly difficult to operate under wartime conditions. As reflected in the near even combat losses in both years, tremendous reinforcement efforts managed to keep the naval air force in contention, but by the time it was finally withdrawn in late 1943 and 1944, irreparable harm had been done. We do not know exactly what casualties were, but if we assume the death of the crew in combat losses and at least one death on average per operational loss, then over this two-year period the JNAF lost at least 6,000 pilots and flight crewmen, not to mention ground crew and other skilled personnel lost to enemy action or disease, or simply left behind in isolated garrisons. The magnitude of this disaster becomes clear when we recall that at the beginning of the war there were only 1,500 trained naval pilots.[20]

This is not to say the naval air force completely disappeared. In 1944 it still had a strength of thousands of planes and pilots, and more than two thousand planes of all types were being manufactured each month by the homeland. But the lack of trained crews and low numbers of more advanced aircraft made it extremely difficult to mount sustained and effective air operations. Unfortunately for Japan, this situation also coincided with great increases in the number and quality of American pilots and planes and the return of fast and powerful U.S. Navy carrier groups to the central Pacific. By late 1943, flying against the Americans was already nearly suicidal. Japanese airmen were more than willing to face death, but by the time of the Leyte landings in 1944 their limited ability to inflict damage on the Americans through conventional air operations was producing widespread despair.[21] It was in this context that the *shimpu,* or special suicide operations program sprang to life.

The kamikaze program is often portrayed as a spontaneous patriotic response from below, by idealistic young officers and their men, to the growing American threat. Whatever its origins, it was quickly seized upon and
orchestrated by incorrigible elements of the higher command who were
willing to bring their country to utter ruin rather than concede defeat, an at-
titude captured in the slogan "One hundred million will die for Emperor
and Nation." From an instrumentalist point of view, however, the postwar
United States Strategic Bombing Survey (USSBS) conclusion that the use of
the kamikazes was "Macabre, effective, supremely practical under the circumstances, supported and stimulated by a powerful propaganda campaign" still seems correct.[22] In the span of a few months the Japanese were
able to develop a formidable and partly successful response to overwhelming American air superiority. Neither collective derangement nor a purely
noble gesture, the *shimpu* air tactics adopted in 1944 were a practical and
relatively efficient method of engaging and inflicting significant losses on
American naval forces at a time when no other method of air attack worked.

The first organized strikes, on a fairly small scale, were directed at American ships in and around Leyte in October of 1944.[23] The possibility of using such tactics, however, had been under discussion for months before-
hand. Once approved, local commanders began to reorganize parts of their
forces for special attacks. Commanders like Vice Admiral Onishi found the
initial results encouraging, both in terms of the number of pilots who managed to crash American ships and the dreadful damage they were capable of
inflicting when they did so, although damage reports were often inflated.
Attacks continued on a larger scale against the American invasion fleet on
its way to the landings at Lingyan Gulf on Luzon. Twenty-five percent of the
kamikazes sent out managed to hit an enemy ship, and one in thirty-three
of those hit sank. Months later, at Okinawa, despite massive countermeasures by the Americans, 32 percent of the kamikaze sorties that managed to
leave their bases succeeded in hitting an Allied ship.[24] This was seven to ten
times the success rate of conventional sorties. During the battle Japanese
airmen established a favorable overall casualty rate against U.S. Navy personnel of 5 to 1, including a 2 to 1 killed in action ratio. By contrast, Japanese ground forces on Okinawa, in one of the hardest fought battles of the
war, managed a killed in action ratio of about 1 to 10. In the earlier battle
of the Philippine Sea, which preceded by several months the adoption of
special attack operations, large-scale conventional attacks against the U.S.
Fleet near Saipan had resulted in the almost total loss of Japanese planes
committed as well as three fleet carriers.[25] Not a single American ship had
been sunk. Clearly the USSBS conclusion that the suicide attacks were "effective" and "supremely practical under the circumstances" was justified.

However dangerous, kamikaze tactics were not in any sense a war-
winning weapon. It was only in combination with other conditions that

they could have significantly contributed to a more successful overall Japanese strategy. First and foremost among those was the avoidance of early strategic errors in the air war. For example, the carrier arm needed to be preserved and expanded as rapidly as possible, rather than thrown away at Midway. The four fleet carriers and hundreds of pilots, crews, and planes lost there would have formed the core element of the fleet in being described in the preceding chapter. The "beaching" of carrier air groups, that is, using highly trained pilots to operate from land bases, where their particular skills quickly deteriorated, should have been prohibited, and the veterans used for intensive training of new groups. The need to avoid disadvantageous attritional air battles over strategically marginal places on the periphery was equally important. This does not mean that outposts like Guadalcanal, Buna, Tarawa, Truk, New Georgia, and Rabaul should have been abandoned without a struggle. But definite limits should have been placed on the level of force committed to their defense. The rationale for such outposts should have been to delay the enemy, force it to deploy its forces, and gain valuable intelligence about how it fought, while conducting a planned withdrawal under air cover from deeper within the empire.

In this context Bergerud's conclusion about how fighting on in the South Pacific created empire-wide defense problems for the Japanese armed forces is salient:

By late summer 1943 it was obvious at Rabaul and Tokyo that Japan's position in the South Pacific was hanging by a thread. In hindsight the Japanese should have seen all too clearly that their delaying campaign in the Solomons and New Guinea was turning into a trap for land garrisons and a place where it would lose priceless aircraft and irreplaceable warships. To slow down MacArthur's drive towards the Philippines. . . . imperial forces were crippling their own ability to confront the new U.S. naval menace, a threat supported by a large and well-trained amphibious force growing daily at Pearl Harbor. Once Lae and New Georgia were lost the Japanese should have done everything possible to withdraw forces from the South Pacific and move them into the Central Pacific and Indies. . . . What the Japanese needed was a redeployment and a period of calm to prepare for the inevitable hurricane brewing in both the Central Pacific and South Pacific. A strategic withdrawal, even if incomplete, would have provided that. . . . It is worth pointing out that Japan had as many men defending Rabaul and Kavieng as they later did on Okinawa. The 250,000 troops in or on their way to New Guinea (not to mention the 100,000 men garrisoning Rabaul, New Ireland, and Bougainville) could have been used to bring major reinforcements to spots like Saipan, Guam, Iwo Jima, Borneo, and Okinawa. At the same time, Japan's deadly destroyer and cruiser force was wasting away in the face of Allied air and naval actions, just as they were needed to hunt submarines and support fleet operations. The Japanese were turning a strategic error into a strategic disaster.[26]

The Japanese were aware that in any long-term struggle with the United States, the weight of American resources and production would eventually be telling. After their initial expansion, hopes for Japanese victory hinged principally on mounting a strong enough resistance that the United States would have been willing to enter into some kind of negotiated settlement which would have preserved vital Japanese gains. But beyond that it was clear that if the Americans were able to penetrate within range of the Home Islands, the war would be lost. What was needed was stricter adherence to Japan's original strategic intent to create an in-depth defense zone to protect the empire from the inevitable American attacks. Emphasis should therefore have been placed on urgent preparation of impregnable defenses in those areas that the Americans could not easily bypass. This was exactly George Marshall's greatest concern—that if given enough time the Japanese could construct strong enough defenses to offset the U.S. superiority in numbers and material—one of the main reasons that he supported Admiral King's plan for an early counteroffensive in the South Pacific.

Besides avoiding needless losses, what was needed in terms of the overall air war was that the attention and resources released by a more limited commitment to the South Pacific be used to build up stronger air defenses deep in the empire. By taking advantage of interior lines and the relative safety of imperial waters in the 1942–1943 period, a dense net of hundreds of interconnected nodal, intermediary, and small emergency airfields could have been constructed and in place before the Americans were able to move against the empire in strength. Dispersal, hardening, hiding, and deception on a large scale would have made possible rapid and flexible multipoint massing of hundreds of land-based planes operating at short ranges over their own territory. The originating points in this system would have been, as they were historically, Japan itself, Korea, Formosa, parts of coastal China, and the Indies, with dense linked networks of land-based airpower deployed on the Marianas and Carolines, Iwo Jima, Okinawa, Western New Guinea, and the Philippines, the very places that had to be denied to the Allies if Japan was to have a chance to avoid overwhelming defeat. Special suicide operations integrated earlier and on a larger scale into exactly such prepared aerial killing grounds could only have resulted in a more effective defense of the empire.

The earlier organization of the kamikaze program would also have maximized the unique blend of resources and techniques that Japan could bring to the air war. Triage of pilot trainees could have directed the most promising into the conventional army and navy air units, while large numbers of less qualified personnel would only receive the minimal training needed for suicide flights. Since trainers, older planes, and even obsolete models were perfectly adequate for the role, there would be no need to use first-line aircraft. Production runs of stripped down older models could have been extended for this purpose. Furthermore, resources devoted to the production of units that had been proven to be terribly vulnerable to Allied attacks in the early months of the war, like multiengine and multicrew bombers, should have immediately been switched to production of advanced higher performance interceptors for conventional air formations.

Kamikaze squadrons themselves, of course, wanted to avoid rather than engage American warplanes. They would have functioned best as in-place, relatively short-ranged additions to the defense of vital places against enemy invasion forces. Launched from hundreds of hiding places, concealed from radar interception by flying directly out of land masses, and rapidly approaching their targets, in large numbers they would have been a formidable weapon against enemy naval units and shipping, as they proved to be later in the war. Earlier organization would have also made possible better training in recognition of enemy ships types and increased their familiarity with the areas they were to operate in, which would have helped avoid the principal targeting problems that plagued special aerial operations later in the war.

Another weakness in the historical kamikaze program was simple lack of numbers, which naturally worked against the tactic of swamping American defenses with continuous attacks. Still, even under near hopeless late war conditions, the Japanese Army and Navy managed to fly around two thousand suicide sorties against Okinawa, and more than five thousand suicide planes and pilots were being prepared for the anticipated invasion of Kyusha in late 1945.[27] So it is not beyond the realm of imagination to suppose that a force of at least ten thousand such suicide planes, or five times the number used at Okinawa, could have easily been organized during 1942 and 1943.

The American military was prepared for most of what it encountered in the Pacific war, but the kamikazes did take it by surprise, and this would have served the Japanese well earlier in the war.[28] Technically speaking, U.S. forces would have been even more unprepared to withstand massive numbers of suicide attacks. Once used on a large scale, the element of surprise would have been lost. The Americans would have quickly instituted countermeasures. But at Okinawa, with the Americans prepared, alert, and enjoying almost complete air superiority, the kamikazes were still able to inflict significant losses.

Japanese forces demonstrated from the beginning to the end of the war their utter devotion to the imperial cause and their absolute determination to fight to the death in its defense. It is therefore no coincidence that even before the organization of kamikaze air attacks, plans were being worked out for other types of suicide missions utilizing manned torpedoes and speedboats filled with high explosives. The acceptance and even the expectation of such heroic measures by Japanese soldiers dated back to the widely publicized 'human cannon ball' episode in the Russo-Japanese War. Once ordered, the cultural climate of the Japanese armed forces would have ensured prompt implementation and enthusiastic participation in such a program. An earlier and larger kamikaze program, well integrated into the deep defenses of the empire, surely would have made U.S. penetration of the empire in 1943 and 1944 less one-sided and more costly than the historical case.

NOTES

1. Descriptions from Morison, *Leyte*, 300–307, 368; *The Liberation of the Philippines*, passim and appendix IV, "Ships Hit or Near Missed and Casualties Inflicted by Kamikaze Attacks in Lingayen Operation, January 1945," 325–26; and *Victory in the Pacific*, passim including appendix II, "United States Ships Sunk or Badly Damaged by Every Action in the Iwo Jima and Okinawa Operation," 389–92. I relied heavily in this chapter on O'Neill, *Suicide Squads*, 118–48; for methods of attack and offense, 133–42; the twenty-second firing window, 137; Okas, 148–62. Another good source on kamikazes is Spector, *At War At Sea*, 292–313. Feifer, *Tennozan*, devotes a chapter to the kamikaze menace on Okinawa, 195–229. See also the extensive coverage in Denis Warner and Peggy Warner, *Sacred Warriors: Japan's Suicide Legions* (New York: Van Nostrand Reinhardt Company, 1984), which includes appendix I, "Kamikaze Score Card From May 1944 to August 14, 1945"; and Ivan Morris, *The Nobility of Failure* (New York: Holt, Rinehart & Winston, 1975).

2. O'Neill, *Suicide Squads*, 143; Feifer, *Tennozan*, 213, 229.

3. O'Neill, *Suicide Squads*, 132–33; Feifer, *Tennozan*, 132–33.

4. For much of what follows I am indebted to the exhaustive study of the 1942 to early 1944 air war by Eric M. Bergerud, *Fire in the Sky*, 5–9; 5–93 for the decisions and actions of the protagonists during this decisive stage of the war.

5. Numbers differ slightly according to the source used. For example, *Reports of General MacArthur*, vol. 2, pt. 1, 56, gives a total of 3,189 first-line airplanes in both services, including 684 carrier types. Numeral discrepancies are caused, for the most part, by different ways of counting specific types of planes—reconnaissance, float planes, etc. Estimates by Dunnigan and Nofi, *Victory at Sea*, 245, 254–56.

6. Bergerud, *Fire in the Sky*, 324–25.

7. Bergerud, *Fire in the Sky*, 328–30; Dunnigan and Nofi, *Victory at Sea*, 254–58; Spector, *At War At Sea*, 140–65.

8. Bergerud, *Fire in the Sky*, 189–225.

9. Ellis, *Brute Force*, 484–95 for production problems.

10. Dunnigan and Nofi, *Victory at Sea*, 245. A fundamental source is two volumes on the history of the army air corps in the Pacific: Wesley F. Craven and James L. Cate, *The Pacific: Guadalcanal to Saipan, August 1942–July 1944* (Chicago: University of Chicago Press, 1950), and *The Pacific: Matterhorn to Nagasaki, June 1944 to August 1945* (Chicago: University of Chicago Press, 1953). Also useful are the reports of General Arnold: Henry H. Arnold, *The War Reports of . . . Marshall . . . Arnold . . . King. Reports of the Commanding General of the Army Air Forces on January 4, 1944, February*

27, 1945, November 12, 1945 (Philadelphia: J. P. Lippincott & Co., 1947); naval aviation is covered in the reports of Admiral King in the same volume.

11. Ellis, *Brute Force*, 485.

12. Dunnigan and Nofi, *Victory at Sea*, 245.

13. Bergerud, *Fire in the Sky*, 227–307. For this and what follows, see James M. Cate and Wesley F. Craven, *The Army Air Forces in World War II: Men and Planes* (Chicago: University of Chicago Press, 1955).

14. Bergerud, *Fire in the Sky*, 330–40; Dunnigan and Nofi, *Victory at Sea*, 256, 330–40; Spector, *At War At Sea*, 140–65, 258–65.

15. Dunnigan and Nofi, *Victory at Sea*, 202–3.

16. Bergerud, *Fire in the Sky*, passim; see 230–33, 407–43 for air combat, 531–656 on destruction of Japanese airbases, and his conclusion, 657–64. Ellis, *Brute Force*, 486, shows virtual parity in front-line aircraft as late as January, 1943.

17. Bergerud, *Fire in the Sky*, 665–66; Spector, *At War At Sea*, 185–204.

18. Bergerud, *Fire in the Sky*, 667–69.

19. Bergerud, *Fire in the Sky*, 670.

20. For the importance of airpower to MacArthur's campaigns, see Griffith, *MacArthur's Airman*, passim.

21. O'Neill, *Suicide Squads*, 119; Spector, *At War At Sea*, 275–86.

22. O'Neill, *Suicide Squads*, 118–32.

23. O'Neill, *Suicide Squads*, 127.

24. O'Neill, *Suicide Squads*, 131–32, 143; Spector, *At War At Sea*, 302, 312.

25. Scorecard in Morison, *Victory in the Pacific*, 319–21; Spector, *At War At Sea*, 275–86; Ellis, *Brute Force*, 488, presents relative losses in a number of campaigns.

26. Bergerud, *Fire in the Sky*, 441.

27. O'Neill, *Suicide Squads*, 143, 236.

28. Dunnigan and Nofi, *Victory at Sea*, 194. The kamikazes' threat prompted a conference at Pearl Harbor in November 1944 by the U.S. Pacific Fleet's high command, resulting in the adoption of wide-ranging countermeasures. O'Neill, *Suicide Squads*, 138.

8

The Japanese Army in the Pacific

When it came, the enemy attack was swift and violent. A preliminary artillery barrage was followed by an air attack from 150 bombers and hundreds of fighters. Then the main artillery bombardment from hundreds of heavy guns came crashing down on Japanese positions. The bombardment continued for hours, expending lavish amounts of ammunition, intermixed with still more strafing and bombing runs by enemy aircraft that seemed to have complete mastery of the skies. Enemy infantry attacked, supported by large numbers of tanks, many terrifyingly equipped with flame-throwers. Those Japanese soldiers who survived the initial assaults fought back from entrenchments and strong points. But their supporting artillery had largely been destroyed, and their light antitank guns found it difficult to knock out enough of the advancing tanks to halt the attack. Infantry assaults penetrated the Japanese lines, isolating the defenders in pockets that were then sealed off and eliminated piecemeal. The Japanese nevertheless fought ferociously. Close combat groups armed with satchel charges, mines, and improvised Molotov cocktails swarmed over the attacking tanks, destroying or disabling many but at great cost to themselves. Their batteries smashed and automatic weapons destroyed, most defenders had only rifles, bayonets, grenades, and their bare hands to use against the attackers, who relentlessly used their massive material superiority over the next few days to destroy the Japanese Army's 23rd Division and occupy its prepared defensive positions.

Such defeat, and indeed annihilation, by superior forces, was to be the ultimate fate of many Japanese defenders during the Pacific War. But the destruction of the 23rd Division actually took place in Manchuria, in 1939, more than two years before the attack on Pearl Harbor. A series of border clashes between the Soviets and the Kwantung Army had escalated into a full-scale conflict. Initial Japanese attacks had been stopped cold by the Soviets who, under the command of the future Marshal Zhukov, went over to the offensive against Japanese forces with more than one million troops and thousands of tanks, guns, and planes. Faced for the first time with the highly mechanized modern forces of a major power instead of the large, underarmed, and poorly led armies of China, the Japanese Army failed the test. It was the 23rd, a first line but fairly new Kwantang Army division entrenched near Nomonhon that bore the brunt of the attack. In slightly more than one week of fighting the division suffered 5,425 killed or missing and 5,455 wounded, a combat casualty rate of 68 percent, which, if 1,340 sick are included, amounted to an overall loss rate of 77 percent, effectively eliminating it as a unit.[1]

The ease with which Soviet tanks, planes, and guns crushed the more lightly equipped Japanese troops sent a shock wave through the Imperial Japanese Army, which had always seen Russia as its major enemy and been training to fight it for decades. Once a cease-fire was in place, a series of investigating committees produced remarkably self-critical reviews of the disaster. Much of the IGHQ final report released in early 1940 focused on technical and organizational issues, particularly the lack of powerful enough antitank guns, the inferiority of Japanese tanks in terms of guns, armor, range, tactical speed, and numbers compared to the Soviets, and the need for heavier artillery with greater range. The report emphasized the need to motorize and to put more firepower into units and to create separate armor divisions. Though it had led to tactical failures and needlessly high casualties, however, the army's emphasis on the use of "spiritual power" to overcome material factors was not challenged, although some officers did advance the notion that it was difficult to defeat an enemy armed with modern weapons if spirit was not combined with favorable material conditions. Some of the report's suggestions were followed, at least in a tentative manner, but for the most part the requisite weapons and vehicles were not produced in large numbers and were introduced to units on a haphazard and piecemeal basis. The Japanese Army that went to war with the Allies in 1941 was essentially the same as the one that had fought at Nomonhon in 1939.[2]

Although the Japanese Army had gone from victory to victory in China and rapidly defeated the white imperialist forces in Southeast Asia, it was ultimately outfought and crushed by American, British, and Commonwealth forces, as well as Soviet forces again at the very end of the war. There are many explanations for this catastrophic failure. The Japanese Army, for example, is often described as a light infantry army, one suited to defeating Chinese forces but ill-equipped compared to the Western armies that had experienced the destructive firepower of modern weaponry in World War I. It also stands accused of a litany of serious flaws: obsession for the offen-

sive, contempt for defense, disregard of logistics, antirational thinking, fanatical suicidal expectations, and a predilection for intra- and interservice
factionalism and rivalry. To a basic miscomprehension of what was to be required to wage a successful modern war was joined an inadequate and
backward industrial and technical base. Starting off behind, the Japanese
Army never caught up.

While all of this is true, there is a different and I believe better explanation for the Japanese Army's failure. In particular it was not its essential nature but the inadequate size and timing of its commitment to the defense
of the Pacific that determined its defeat. There were, from a counterfactual
point of view, opportunities to have used the army more effectively that, if
they had been taken, could have contributed significantly to altering the
face of the war in the Pacific. A larger and more timely use of the army
would have created much more favorable conditions to stop the American
advance, for the army had the numbers, weapons, and fighting prowess to
have fought much more successfully, particularly in the central Pacific. In
many ways the Japanese Army defeated itself in the Pacific as much as it was
defeated by the United States.

Even though it is true that the Japanese Army was hampered by institutional and technical weaknesses throughout the Pacific war, these are not in
and of themselves sufficient to explain the abject depth of defeat, even in
the face of overwhelming force developed in the end by the Allies. From a
technical point of view, for example, Japanese weaponry, properly em-
placed, was quite adequate against the primarily infantry forces that led the
assaults against the beaches and prepared defenses of the empire—as the
ghastly casualty lists of U.S. Marine and Army combat units show.[3] The lack
of heavy artillery was a real disadvantage, but could be and partly was reme-
died by larger numbers of lighter guns and mortars. The inadequacies of
Japanese tanks—one of the most frequently cited lessons of Nomonhon—
and the failure to produce larger numbers of improved models like the
other great powers can hardly stand as an adequate explanation of why
Japan lost the war. In China, and during the Malaya campaign, the Japanese used armor to good effect, but most of the terrain and places that had
to be defended in the Pacific, with few exceptions, did not lend themselves
at all to the widespread employment of armored formations. One could indeed argue that the resources devoted to the few inadequate tanks that were
actually produced by Japan would have been more profitably invested in
bulldozers and other earthmovers.

Furthermore, as antirational as their extreme emphasis on the importance of the offensive was, disdain for the defense did not prevent Japanese
commanders, troops, and combat engineers from building some of the
most effective stationary defenses ever seen in war. The war in fact witnessed
a continually escalating contest between Japanese defenders and American

weaponry. The American forces that fought on Guadalcanal were almost every bit a light infantry army as the Japanese. The introduction of armed and armored amphibious assault craft and vehicles, heavier artillery, rocket-firing close support vessels, and more powerful tanks operating in an infantry support role, as well as tremendous increases in the number of automatic weapons, explosive charges, flame throwers, and bazookas used by American assault troops were necessary to overcome Japanese defenses that increased in depth and thickness by going underground, becoming invisible and nearly impervious to air or artillery bombardment.[4] Peleliu, Iwo Jima, and Okinawa were perfect examples of the kind of hardened defenses and skilled and fanatical resistance that the Japanese Army units were capable of. And though brutal discipline, thoughtless obedience, and acceptance or insistence on fighting to the death, along with a chronic lack of tactical coordination and hopeless counterattacks often produced tragedies and absurdities, they also produced some of the most formidable, tenacious, toughest, and ferocious combat infantry of the war, as any Allied soldier who fought in the Pacific or Southeast Asia could attest. Every day, ordinary defending Japanese soldiers routinely did things that would have earned them a medal for valor in any Allied army.[5]

The problem with battles like Iwo Jima and Okinawa was not that they were lost, but that they were lost on the doorstep of the homeland. What was needed was more battles like them farther away from the core of the empire and earlier in the war. Japan entrusted the defense of the Pacific to the imperial navy for far too long. The Japanese Army should have been introduced in massive numbers and prepositioned to defend the Pacific early in the war. For it was the limited number of Imperial Japanese Army (IJA) troops in the Pacific and the belated and poor timing of their commitment, not weaponry, banzai tactics, or even necessarily poor logistics, that led to the loss of absolutely key positions. Nowhere is this more evident than in the Marianas in the summer of 1944.

The fall of the Marianas, especially Saipan, was one of the greatest military disasters of the war for Japan. Indeed, it could be argued that it constituted the single most pivotal event in her defeat. Certainly from the beginning of the war Admiral King thought that the way to victory lay in making the Marianas the principal target of a central Pacific drive by the U.S. Navy. But it took some time before the taking of the Marianas became an important American goal. U.S. strategic policies and priorities were constantly evolving in the Pacific in response to events. For some time it was not clear if the United States would implement some form of the prewar versions of Plan Orange: an advance by the Pacific Fleet through the Mandates to the Philippines where it could fight a decisive battle with the Japanese Navy and then mount a close blockade against the Home Islands. Successes in the Solomons and New Guinea in fact for a time suggested that a westward

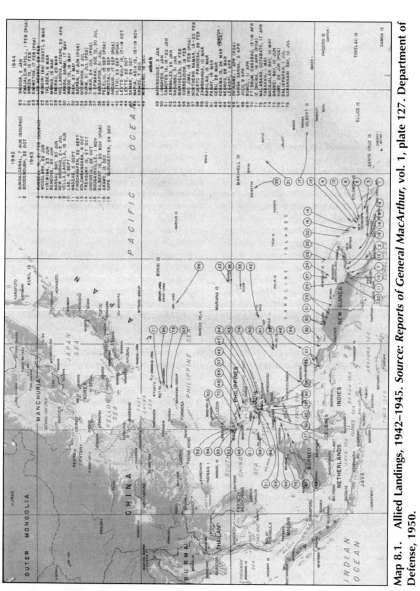

Map 8.1. Allied Landings, 1942–1945. *Source: Reports of General MacArthur*, vol. 1, plate 127. Department of Defense, 1950.

drive along New Guinea to the Philippines might be the best way to cut Japanese access to its Southeast Asian resource base. Another possibility was to operate through the central Pacific to seize Formosa and areas on the Asian mainland so that the United States could equip the seemingly endless manpower resources of China for use against Japan. The United States finally decided to use the growing numbers of newly completed American warships and the fast developing amphibious capabilities of the Pacific Fleet to start the central Pacific drive that began with the assault on Tarawa in late 1943. This central thrust was to be given priority as the best and quickest route to the defeat of Japanese naval and air forces. MacArthur nevertheless was to continue his drive along the New Guinea coast, threatening the Indies and the Philippines, and forcing the Japanese to stretch themselves thin in order to meet both threats.

The ultimate goal of the central advance was initially left rather vague—only the strategic triangle China-Formosa-Philippines was specified. But the unexpectedly rapid advance through the Gilberts and the Marshalls, which with the exception of Tarawa were weakly defended, and the aerial neutralization of Truk, brought the Marianas back into the strategic picture. Admiral King's vision of their crucial importance was now supported by General Arnold, the commander of the army air force, who wanted the islands because they would bring Japan within range of his new B-29 heavy bombers. In fairly short order all this came together—the Marianas were seized in the summer of 1944 and in November, XXI Bomber Command began flying missions against Japan. When MacArthur persuaded the Joint Chiefs to use his forces and those of the Pacific Fleet together to begin the liberation of the Philippines in October 1944, landings on Formosa or China were dropped as beyond the logistical capabilities of American forces in the Pacific. Instead, Nimitz's forces seized Iwo Jima and Okinawa in the spring and summer of 1945 to be used, along with Luzon, as the major staging areas for the invasion of Japan that General Marshall was convinced would be necessary to overcome Japanese resistance and bring the war in the East to a close.

Part of the Mandates granted to Japan by the League of Nations in 1922, the Marianas are a four hundred-mile long chain of islands running generally south of the Bonin Islands and northeast of the Philippines. Saipan, its neighbor Tinian, and Guam one hundred miles to their south, are the largest islands in the lower part of the chain. Guam was under American control until seized by Japanese forces at the beginning of the war. Saipan's importance sprang from its central position on the most eastward of the major north-south convoy routes that connected Japan with its possessions and conquests in the Pacific.[6] From the Marianas the route went on to Truk, the main imperial navy base in the central Pacific, and from there south to Rabaul or east to the Marshall and Gilbert Islands. Aside from the value of its modest port and airfield facilities, it was an obvious stepping-stone for any enemy advance northward on Honshu by way of Iwo Jima and one of the only places in the central Pacific that was within B-29 range of Japan.

Despite its obvious strategic importance, however, Saipan had largely remained a backwater after the fighting moved thousands of miles to the south. Rather than seizing the window of opportunity provided by the relative safety of shipping routes from enemy submarine and air attack in 1942–1943 to prepare it to withstand the enemy, its defenses were totally neglected, like those of many other key positions in the Pacific before 1944. Even after the fall of the Solomons and Papua New Guinea to the Allies and its designation in September 1943 as a vital part of the IGHQ's new absolute zone of national defense, most of its defending troops arrived in May 1944, just weeks before the American attack. By that time the Americans had already raced through the Gilbert and Marshall Islands, neutralized Truk—forcing the Combined Fleet to retreat to Borneo—and chosen June 15 as D-Day for Saipan.

As a recent history of the campaign notes:

> The larger hilly islands in the Marianas provided the opportunity to establish defenses in greater depth in multiple lines, develop strongpoints on key terrain, and allow centrally positioned reserves to maneuver to counterattack. The Japanese were unable to take advantage of most of these factors, however. Sufficient forces did not arrive on the islands until less than two months before the US assault. This did not allow adequate time to prepare inland defenses in multiple lines. Numerous coast defense and AA guns were found still in their packing beside unfinished positions. Insufficient construction materials were available to build hardened positions. As it was, the high ground on the island's center had not been prepared for defense and many of the beach defenses were not complete.[7]

Altogether more than 25,000 army and 6,000 navy personnel, the equivalent of about two reinforced divisions, had reached Saipan before June 15. But these numbers are completely misleading, for many formations had taken losses of men and equipment from submarine attacks, a large number of troops belonged to shipping, labor, and air service units, while others, separated from their parent units, were trapped on the island while in transit. The 43rd division, which was intended to form the backbone of the defenses, lost five of the seven transports carrying its second echelon and though many personnel were rescued, the 118th infantry regiment, which lost 1,400 men and all its equipment, was no longer an effective unit. By the time the entire division was assembled, its strength was down to 12,900 men with no organic artillery. The 18th regiment of the 29th division, sailing for Guam at the end of February, lost more than half of its 3,000 troops and all its weapons and equipment to torpedoes. Only 600 shocked survivors, organized into a single battalion on Saipan, were capable of fighting. The artillery on the island, bereft of vehicles or horses, could only be moved by hand. Of the 25,000 army troops on the island, only 19,000 were armed and more than 4,000 stragglers roamed back areas. More than 2,000 of the naval troops on the island manned coastal batteries placed around the perimeter of the island. Most of those batteries, and all the planes on the island, were destroyed by air raids or naval bombardment at the beginning of the battle. The Yokosaka 1st Special Naval Landing Forces (SNLF), formerly a parachute battalion, and now at half strength, was the only properly trained naval infantry force on the island. The remaining sailors, mostly headquarter and airfield personnel, untrained and poorly armed, were organized into provisional rifle battalions. There were not enough troops to defend the beaches and to form a substantial tactical reserve in the interior of the island.[8]

Even so, for the one Army and two U.S. Marine divisions, totaling about sixty-seven thousand assault troops, the fight for Saipan was long and hard. The Americans suffered two thousand casualties on the first day alone and were forced to begin landing their floating reserve Army division on D+1. Their attempts to link up their separate bridgeheads and clear the island of Japanese defenders from south to north met constant fanatical resistance from defenders dug in or hiding in the varied and rugged terrain of the island. Many U.S. battalions suffered such high casualties that they had to be pulled out of combat. The concurrent invasion of Guam, originally planned for June 18, had to be indefinitely postponed. Nevertheless the Americans, supported by medium tanks and overwhelming artillery and close air support, slowly fought their way forward, pressing the defenders back into the northern tip of the island. From there on the morning of July 8 the few thousand surviving Japanese launched a final banzai attack, overrunning one Marine Artillery and two U.S. infantry battalions and inflicting over one thousand casualties before they were finally destroyed. American troops were also confronted in the last days with the horrific deaths of thousands of Japanese civilians who committed mass suicide or were murdered by Japanese troops to prevent their capture. Saipan was declared secure on July 9, though hundreds of survivors remained to surrender or be hunted down during the mop-up phase.[9]

Over the course of more than three weeks of fighting the American assault forces suffered 16,525 combat casualties including 3,426 killed and 13,099 wounded, an overall loss rate (not counting sailors or the sick) of 24.5 percent. Approximately 29,500 Japanese defenders were killed and 1,790 (half of whom were Koreans) captured. All 32,000 defenders, in other words, became casualties.[10] But although outnumbered, unprepared, and underarmed, they had caused one American casualty for every two of their own, and one enemy fatality for every ten defenders killed during the desperate resistance. In Japan the fall of Saipan was widely regarded as evidence that the war was lost, and Tojo and his cabinet, who had been in charge of the Japanese war effort from the beginning, were forced to resign. Even before the fighting finished, construction of airfields had begun and in November, XXI Bomber Command began B-29 attacks on Japan. The planes bearing the atomic bombs that ended the war the following summer flew from nearby Tinian island.

In almost all important respects, the loss of Saipan can serve as an iconic example of the inability of the Japanese Army to prevent the Americans from storming key positions in the Pacific during 1944 and 1945. Exactly the same kinds of factors that compromised the defense of Saipan figured prominently both before and later in the losses of other places. Of those most important was a simple lack of numbers. Japan had a large army: some 50 divisions were serving abroad at the beginning of the war while an additional 117 who also served abroad were raised during the war. Another 56 divisions, most of them raised in Japan at the end of the war to defend against the expected American invasion, brought the grand total to 223 divisions.[11] The undermechanized aspects of the army meant not only that defensive preparations, but also actually fighting the Americans was an extremely labor intensive endeavor. Numbers of properly trained troops were therefore of crucial importance. In fact, the level of casualties inflicted on American forces in the battles of 1944–1945 was closely related to the size of defending Japanese forces.

Although willing to suffer enormous casualties to take key positions, the Americans strategically preferred not to fight large portions of the IJA if they could be avoided. Yet for the first two critical years of the war, Japanese defenses in the Pacific were starved of experienced infantry formations. Figure 8.1, which tracks by month the number of divisional size Japanese Army units deployed in the Pacific from the beginning of the Guadalcanal campaign to the end of the war, vividly illustrates this limited and belated commitment. At the beginning of the war the Japanese Army committed eleven divisions, about one fifth of its strength, to the great southern advance; the rest remained in China and Manchuria. Of those eleven divisions three campaigned in the south and central Pacific. At the time of the American landings on Guadalcanal, only two army divisions were stationed in the areas that would later bear the brunt of the Allied advance. So, while the bulk of the army remained focused on the Asian mainland, particularly China, the defense of the Pacific was left to the Japanese Navy, its air force, and a limited number of its naval infantry units. As can be seen, by the end of August 1942 the army had committed four divisions to the Solomons and Papua New Guinea campaigns, much less than ten percent of its total strength. And though twelve new divisions, including three armor divisions, were added to the empire-wide total during 1942, they remained on

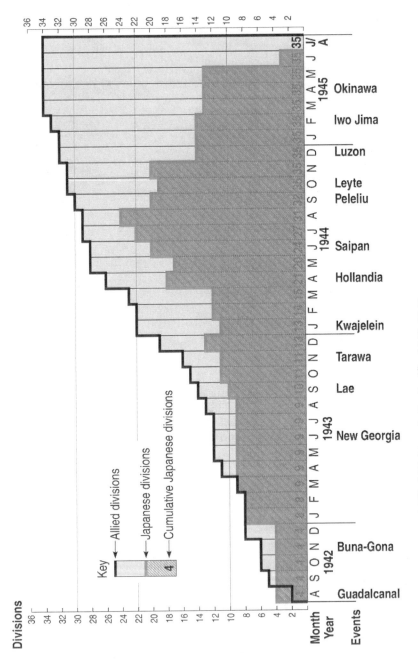

Figure 8.1. Japanese and Allied Divisions in the Pacific, 1942–1945.

the mainland. Only in January of 1943 were four more, and in May, one more veteran division sent to the Pacific. So from August 1942 to August 1943 only nine Japanese Army divisions served in the Pacific, most in the Solomons or Papua New Guinea where they were isolated or destroyed by MacArthur and Halsey's forces. What is noteworthy is that the Allies, even in what was for them the most desperate time of the war, managed to have from one to three more divisions in the Pacific area than the Japanese. By January 1944 the number of Allied divisions had grown to twenty-one and by October to thirty-one. The Japanese Army finally began dispatching more divisions to the Pacific when the new National Defense Zone was proclaimed in September 1943, doubling their numbers to twenty-four, their highest cumulative total, in the fall of 1944. But this nominal increase in the number of Japanese divisions is misleading, for as we saw in the Saipan case, many of the divisions sent to the Pacific had suffered losses on the way to their new stations and most were inserted into poorly prepared defenses only weeks or months before American landings took place. By the end of the war a cumulative total of thirty-five divisions, almost all of them prewar formations, but still only about one fifth of the total number of Japanese Army divisions that served overseas, had been dispatched to the Pacific. But all of them had been destroyed or isolated while the thirty-four Allied divisions that served in the Pacific were still active and at near full strength at the end of the war.[12]

Every major Japanese defeat on land in 1944–1945, not just Saipan, was due in part to lack of numbers and lack of time to prepare proper defenses. On Leyte there were not enough troops to man both the formidable beach defenses and the main inland lines of resistance. The defense of Luzon was deeply compromised by the siphoning off of major portions of its garrison, too late to be decisive, to the fighting on Leyte. The best division of troops that the defenders of Okinawa were counting on was ordered to Leyte just four months before the American landings and never replaced. Everywhere important portions of defenses had to be manned by noncombat units, often labor and supply troops who were unskilled and inadequately armed. The Japanese demonstrated an astonishing ability to organize new or rebuild shattered units with such soldiers, but they were no substitute for well-trained and equipped regular units manning hardened defenses. By mid-1944, some 250,000 surviving troops who could have been used to strengthen the National Defense Zone had already been bypassed and left to their fate.

Ironically, the key areas that had been in Japanese hands since early in 1942 were little more prepared to defend themselves than those farther forward. As the Americans advanced, the atolls of the central Pacific were replaced by far larger and more rugged islands that were perfectly suited for defense. Having learned not to depend entirely on stopping the landings on the beaches themselves, the Japanese began digging in deeper and further inland, taking advantage of demanding terrain, cave systems, high ground, and reverse slopes to build multiple lines of resistance based on mutually supporting pillboxes, bunkers, strong points, and artillery. Iwo Jima, Pelieu, and Okinawa are perhaps the best examples of such defenses. But despite the fact that most of Dutch New Guinea had been in Japanese hands for more than two years, the Allies managed to advance to its western tip, within striking range of the Philippines, before it could be put in an effective state of defense. The American advance through the Gilberts and Marshalls after Tarawa encountered only very weak defenses despite the fact that the area had been part of the Japanese Mandate well before the war began. The ability to advance quickly through the central Pacific was critically important to the Americans. Lack of resistance allowed them to advance assault landing dates by using uncommitted reserves while raids by their carrier forces and the increasing effectiveness of their submarines meant they could neutralize Truk, already fatally weakened by its contributions to the defense of Rabaul, rather than invade it. The sudden fall of Kwajelein allowed the assault on Eniwietok to take place in February rather than May 1944, while the date for the invasion of Saipan was advanced five months to June 15. Chronic indefensibility thus allowed the Americans to concentrate a sufficient number of their slender forces to seize each key position that was needed to continue their advance. With their fleet unable to operate, their air power decimated, and kamikaze force only beginning to be organized in late 1944, Japanese soldiers had to fight at a great disadvantage in the complicated rock-scissors-paper game that the war in the Pacific had become.

Despite these disadvantages, however, the Japanese resisted the Allied advance tenaciously everywhere that they came to grips with it. The continuous amphibious assault tactics adopted by the Americans, especially in the central Pacific, played right into the hands of Japanese defenders who wanted nothing more than the chance to cause as many casualties as they could before their own death. Even when Japanese defenses and tactics were inadequate, land fighting in the close quarters of Pacific battlefields caused such shockingly high casualties that American assault divisions needed months to regain their effectiveness after an operation. It is hard not to wonder just how much more effective Japanese resistance could have been if the army from the beginning of the war had poured its numbers, energy, combat experience, and engineering skills into construction and manning of the National Defense Zone as it had originally been envisioned.

Furthermore there was at least a twelve-month window of opportunity during which conditions were highly favorable for a much more sizeable army buildup in the Pacific. Twenty additional full divisions deployed and in place before mid-1943 would have greatly altered the conditions under which the Allies had to carry out their advance. Nor would the China or Manchuria theaters been seriously weakened by removal of units during this early period. The battles for Saipan, Leyte, and Luzon would certainly have been longer and harder if they had contained adequate numbers of Japanese troops, weapons, and significantly stronger defenses. And in the second half of 1943 and early 1944, at a singularly critical moment in the preparations for the assault on Nazi-occupied Europe, would the Americans have been willing to press their advance if every place they invaded caused losses on a larger scale than at Tarawa or Peleliu, prefiguring Okinawa? The degree to which Japanese Army defenders in the Pacific were able to inflict high casualties on the enemy during this period was directly proportional to the number of troops deployed and the state of their defenses. More troops and better-prepared defenses could have greatly multiplied Japanese fighting effectiveness. American troops on Okinawa broke down when they had to endure concentrated heavy artillery bombardments for the first time while Japanese defenders, despite the inadequacy of their weapons, managed to destroy 153 of some 350 medium tanks deployed there by the Americans.[13] Indeed the resistance encountered in 1945 was so fierce that the American Chiefs of Staff seriously considered reintroducing poison gas to use against Japanese defenders.[14] Based on their experience of fighting the Japanese, the Americans anticipated such high losses during the upcoming November invasion of Kyushu that Admirals King and Nimitz were ready to withdraw U.S Navy support for the operation.[15]

These mid- and late-war battles should and could have been fought thousands of miles farther away from Japan. In football parlance, the Japanese needed one or two good defensive stands to upset the delicate interdependencies of the American operational calendar and significantly slow the speed of their advance. The resources and time needed to create more favorable defensive conditions in the Pacific were there for a period, but the opportunity was missed to prevent or at least significantly postpone such critical events as the fall of Saipan or the loss of the Philippines.

Obviously a larger and earlier presence of the army would not in and of itself have automatically led to a more effective Japanese defense of the Pacific. The army's defensive potency was closely bound up with what was going on in the other areas of the Japanese war effort that we have analyzed in previous chapters. If American carriers and amphibious forces were still able to come and go as they pleased, an earlier infusion of imperial army troops may have simply led to larger numbers of isolated, bypassed, and ignored defenders and useless defenses. Throwing more troops into Guadalcanal or Papua New Guinea, for example, or continuing to feed reinforcements into Rabaul after it had been neutralized would not have contributed much to the more important and basic project of defending the inner empire. On the other hand, larger and earlier commitments to the Gilberts, Marshalls, Carolines, and Marianas could have had a potentially high payoff. In the Marshalls, besides denying the Pacific Fleet important anchorages for a longer period and complicating its attacks on Truk, more effective re-sistance would have prevented a Marianas invasion five months earlier than had originally been planned. The Carolines were also a key area in the ap-proaches to the empire. Ulithi, which became the most important forward base and anchorage of the Pacific Fleet, was actually evacuated by the Japan-ese shortly before the Americans seized it. The Marianas and the Philippines could certainly have profited from much larger defending forces. Even New Guinea might have been defended for longer against Allied forces if the Japanese had concentrated on early creation of a dense complex of airfields and bases linked with a viable coastal road on her western end.

Such partial delays imposed on the Americans could have had much wider reverberations. It is hard not to wonder if a later American invasion of a better defended Saipan might have failed. Even its fall in December rather than July 1944 would have had important repercussions. Historically it took the Americans four months of construction and buildup before the first B-29 raids were launched against Japan. It then took another four months for them to build up their bomber strength, gain experience of the air defenses and unfavorable weather and stratospheric conditions over Japan, and conclude that their high altitude bombing of industrial targets was not having enough success. After they switched to low-level incendiary attacks on Japan's cities, it took another five months to reduce them to rub-ble.[16] Had this whole complicated process had to begin in December 1944, the first effective strategic bombing of Japan would not have commenced until August 1945, and Japan's cities would not have reached their histori-cal level of destruction until January 1946. Under these conditions the No-vember 1945 invasion would have required postponement to a later date. It is true that the first operational A-bombs would still have been ready in August 1945, but with Japanese cities and industry virtually unharmed and only one or two new bombs being produced monthly, the effect of their use and the potential impact on Japanese leadership might have been consid-erably different. A successful defeat of an American invasion of Saipan would have had an even greater impact. The war in the Pacific could hardly have followed its historical path if at the beginning of 1945 the Americans had not reached the inner defenses of the empire, were in no position for a strategic bombing campaign, had no prospects of invading Japan until 1946, and faced the possibility of being bled white by the hardened de-fenses that awaited them there.

NOTES

1. For a highly detailed account of the 23rd Division's destruction, Coox, *Nomon-han*, 663–841; division casualties on 915–16.

2. On the search for scapegoats which produced voluntary and forced suicides, Coox, *Nomonhan*, 952–79; for the investigation and outcome, 991–1032; and Edward J. Drea, "Tradition and Circumstances: The Imperial Japanese Army's Tactical Response to Khalkhin-Gol, 1939," in Drea, *In the Service of the Emperor*, 1–13.

3. For a contemporary guide to Japanese forces see U.S. War Department, TM-E20-430, *Handbook on Japanese Forces* (Washington, DC: GPO, 1944), reprint edition (Baton Rouge: Louisiana State University Press, 1991), with a new introduction by David C. Isby. Leo J. Daugherty, III, *Fighting Techniques of a Japanese Infantryman, 1941–1945: Training Techniques and Weapons* (St. Paul, MN: MBI Publishing Company, 2002) provides a clear and well-informed description of how the army fought. For army strategy, Hayashi, *Kōgun*; Drea, "Imperial Japanese Army Strategy and the Pacific War (1941–45)" in *In the Service of the Emperor*, 26–41; and Coox, "Japanese Military Effectiveness," in Williamson and Murray, *Military Effectiveness*, vol. 3, 1–44.

4. Gordon L. Rottman, *Japanese Pacific Island Defenses, 1941–45* (Oxford, UK: Osprey Publishing, 2003) covers the evolving nature of Japanese defenses.

5. See Drea, *In the Service of the Emperor*, 75–90, on 'the hard school' of training; Gilmore's marvelous *You Can't Fight Tanks with Bayonets* on the psychology, beliefs, and morale of Japanese soldiers, especially her concluding chapter, 146–79; Gerald F. Lindeman, *The World Within War, America's Combat Experience in World War II* (New York: The Free Press, 1997) on how Japanese "no-surrender" and mass suicidal behavior shaped the Pacific battlefield. On the complicated but irreconcilable nature of Japanese resistance, see the interesting study by Charlotte Carr-Gregg, *Japanese Prisoners of War in Revolt: The Outbreaks at Featherston and Cowra During World War II* (New York: St. Martin's Press, 1978). And though I disagree with some of his conclusions, Cameron, *American Samurai*, 89–129, for U.S. Marine attitudes toward their enemy and the increasing intensity of combat on Peleliu and Okinawa, 130–202. Bergerud, *Touched With Fire*, passim, describes combat in the southwest Pacific in great detail. Oscar E. Gilbert, *Marine Tank Battles in the Pacific* (Conshohocken, PA: Combined Publishing, 2001) provides vivid accounts of the bitterness of fighting. Feifer, *Tennozan*, passim, for the fighting on Okinawa, especially, the involvement of civilians.

6. Besides Morison, *New Guinea and the Marianas*, and Crowl, *Campaign in the Marianas*, much of what follows is drawn from Rottman, *Saipan & Tinian, 1944*.

7. Rottman, *Saipan & Tinian*, 20.

8. Rottman, *Saipan & Tinian*, 18–24, 38–42.

9. Rottman, *Saipan & Tinian*, 52, 68–69.

10. Rottman, *Saipan & Tinian*, 88–89.

11. Ellis, *World War II: The Encyclopedia*, 186–98.

12. Comings and goings tracked in Ellis, *World War II: The Encyclopedia*, 186–98.

13. Rottman, *Okinawa 1945*, 45–46.

14. Frank, *Downfall*, 143.

15. Frank, *Downfall*, 146–47.

16. For the teething difficulties see Werell, *Blankets of Fire*, passim.

Conclusion

The Road Not Taken

With a quick and elegant motion, the Japanese officer drew his ancient samurai sword, whirling on his horse. The column of troops, long bayonets glittering in the sun, snapped to attention, rising sun flags unfurled. Menacingly and methodically the soldiers, eight abreast, began to march, their triumphant and contemptuous expressions in sharp contrast to the ashen faces of the crowds of enemy civilians who lined the roads, witnesses to the conquerors' victory parade down Pennsylvania Avenue to the White House. There humiliating articles of surrender waited to be signed by the remnants of the American government and armed forces. The cruel occupation had begun.

It was, of course, quite impossible that such an event could have come to pass during World War II. But something very similar was forcefully portrayed in filmmaker Frank Capra's 1942 Academy Award–winning *Prelude to War*, part of the propaganda series, *Why We Fight*. In the film Japanese troops victoriously make their way down Pennsylvania Avenue in Washington, DC, while the narrator explains: "You will see what they did to the men and women of Nanking, Hong Kong, and Manila. Imagine the field day they'd enjoy if they marched through the streets of Washington." The scene was an unambiguous reminder to Americans of why they fought, and the consequences of defeat by a savage, cruel, and racially menacing enemy.[1]

There were many reasons for Americans to feel panicky in the early months of the war, but Japanese conquest of the continental United States was not one of them. American military leaders believed that Japan did not pose an immediate mortal danger to the Allies. Despite Japan's dramatic early victories in Asia and the Pacific, she was not considered to have a large enough industrial base to support the level of forces needed to sustain a lengthy war of material against the economic goliath United States. As for the defeat of Japan, it was simply a matter of when, not if, it would happen. Germany was by far the most dangerous foe after an impressive string of conquests that had brought most of the vast resources of western and eastern Europe under her control even before Pearl Harbor. The question was whether any forces at all should be committed to the Pacific before the mobilization of American industrial and military potential had enabled her to defeat Germany.

Of course, between the polar opposites of Japanese occupation of Washington, DC, and swift and total destruction of Japan and her empire by Allied forces, there was a wide continuum of possible historical outcomes. Was one of these outcomes that Japan could win the war? As the war was fought, of course, the answer must be no, for Japan was overwhelmingly defeated. And here the materialistic argument bears some weight. War on American terms, especially a war based on industrial production and technology levels, was bound to end in Japan's defeat. But the Pacific War was more than a war of production capacities. There were many critical arenas of engagement—grand strategy, strategy, operations, and tactics—in which human decisions and judgments remained paramount. After her initial defeats the United States fought a brilliant war in the Pacific—virtually flawless in obtaining its overall objectives. The Japanese conducted a brilliant opening campaign but thereafter a war that increasingly played into American hands. An honest assessment of the course of the Pacific War has to acknowledge that the magnitude of American victory was directly related to Japanese mistakes and missed opportunities. The lost opportunities meant that Japan was condemned to fight a war that was unnecessarily wasteful of men, planes, and ships. Her frontline forces were decimated as much by isolation, lack of medical care, undernourishment, bad maintenance, and vulnerable sea lanes and airfields as by combat casualties. All of these conditions could have been modified in Japan's favor.

Richard Overy writes that:

> On the face of things, no rational man in early 1942 would have guessed at the eventual outcome of the war. . . . The situation for the Allies—and the coalition only emerged in December 1941, not sooner—was desperate, demoralizing . . . [but] Between 1942 and 1944 the initiative passed to the Allies, and Axis forces experienced their first serious reverses. . . . By 1944 the demoralization of the Allies was dispelled; contemporaries could see that the odds were now overwhelmingly on Allied victory.[2]

This was certainly true of the Pacific War: the period of late 1943–1944 saw a surge of American victories that brought her forces to the very doorstep of the inner empire, poised to destroy the Japanese homeland itself. But while this period marked the turning point of the war in the Pacific and the elimination of any hope of Japanese victory, the key to this outcome was what had occurred during 1941 to 1943. During this time the Japanese had many chances to create the conditions that any kind of victory would depend on and at the very least to have laid the groundwork to fight a much more effective and extended war resulting in a *status quo ante* outcome acceptable to both sides. There certainly was, in other words, a window of opportunity for Japan, but once it closed, chances of Japanese victory rapidly faded.

Could Japan have won the Pacific War? Certainly not in the classical sense of a complete military triumph over her enemies. Nevertheless the course the war took was not set in stone from beginning to end. Chance, for example, sometimes intervened, and it took the sustained and cumulative effect of many kinds of forces and actions to shape the unfolding and crystallization of the Pacific War as a large and complex historical event. Many of those forces were at some point susceptible to human control and decisions. But since 1945 historians have largely neglected the fact that different decisions and actions with realistic chances of implementation might have guided the war down alternative pathways. The might of the United States, never even fully applied in the Pacific, and the depth of Japanese defeat, have become woven into a seamless and monolithic historical narrative—tragic in Japanese and triumphant in English.

The goal of this book's extended argument has been to unravel rather than cut through the Gordian knot of our conventional historical understanding of the war in the Pacific by examining the alternative roads that existed at the time even if they were not taken. We began by analyzing why Japan went to war and why the war that she fought led to her defeat. We identified the most important military outcomes that would have had to have been altered or reversed if Japan's defense of her expanded Pacific empire was to be more successful. We held each of these crucial components of military performance—shipping, submarines, the navy, air forces, and army—up to the light of strategic and counterfactual analysis and estimated the range of possible impacts on the war if the Japanese had followed alternative courses in any of those areas.

The reader will by now have decided if the evidence and arguments advanced in each discrete chapter are convincing examples of how the Japanese could have waged a more effective war—not in the best of all possible worlds, but in that specific historical midcentury world. A different course of action in any one of these areas may not by itself have had the dramatic war-winning effect of, say, the atomic bomb. But there were important inherent synergetic possibilities in a different series of military choices. Imposition of a convoy system, for example, could have resulted in safer military passage for troops, equipment, and supplies as well as sustained Japan's industrial output for a longer period of time. A submarine offensive against American shipping would have had a major impact on the ability of the Allies to mount their early counteroffensive in the South Pacific. Construction of a stronger national defense zone would have multiplied the threat and effectiveness of Japanese land-based airpower. Avoidance of overexpansion could have preserved the Combined Fleet's battle and carrier forces for a decisive blow on the Pacific Fleet if it ventured into Japanese controlled waters. Earlier employment and integration of mass kamikaze attacks into imperial defenses would have improved Japanese capabilities to counter and defeat some of the key Allied amphibious assaults. Stronger army involvement in the Pacific would have made Japanese land defenses significantly more difficult to overcome, upset the Allies' opportunistic operational schedule, and delayed the strategic bombing of Japan.

All of these counterfactual possibilities share certain commonalities. First of all, they represent actual choices that were recognized and advocated by at least some among Japan's military leadership. Most were discussed and some were even adopted, though too late to make a significant difference. Air visionaries called for massive expansions in pilot training even before the war. Submarine officers protested their strict subordination to the surface fleet and the diversion of their boats into troop transport and supply operations. The army opposed the "victory disease" expansion that prevented the implementation of the originally quite viable plan for defending Japan's acquisitions. The Navy Chief of Staff fought tooth and nail on solid military grounds against Yamamoto's headstrong Midway adventure. Army and navy officers called for the use of suicide missions more than a year before they were finally adopted. Recognition of the existence of alternatives, in other words, was well within the intellectual capabilities and cultural understanding of the Japanese high command.

A second commonality is that the Allies themselves realized that different courses of action in those areas would have made their path through the Pacific harder and longer and were genuinely concerned that the Japanese would seize such opportunities. The U.S. Navy was amazed that after Pearl Harbor there was no sustained submarine campaign against their very vulnerable communications from the West Coast to Hawaii and to the South Pacific and Australia. American military leaders feared that Japan would complete exactly the kind of fortified national defense zone that her original strategic plan had called for before the Americans were able to build up the necessary strength to attack the empire. The Allies knew that for some significant period of time they were simply not going to be in position to interfere with such initiatives if Japan adopted them. Such Allied fears underline the importance and the pragmatic nature of the alternatives set forth in this book.

A third notable commonality is that in all of these crucial areas the opportunities to construct more successful long-range war policies were to a great extent linked to their implementation in the early period of the war. It took time to introduce and bring such measures to fruition. Lead time, more than material constraints, was the most important factor governing Japanese defense of the Pacific, for the potential cumulative impact of a different military policy was tied to its aggregate operational effects over time. The Japanese tried to introduce measures like convoying and construction of numerous airfields and to move additional forces into the Pacific. To their dismay such efforts did not lead to decisive successes because the necessary preparations that would make them effective were wholly or partially incomplete. But once the window of opportunity closed, it could never be reopened. The Allies swept through or around their objectives before Japanese forces were ready to offer effective, that is, winning resistance. Because Japan's defensive system remained so incomplete and shallow, it was typically logistical constraints rather than the problem of overcoming consistently effective military resistance that governed the speed of the Allied advance.

Bad timing also squandered another important advantage—that until well into 1943, Japan's enemies were too far away to have prevented modifications in Japan's defensive plans. Japan's war-waging decisions were entirely in her own hands. But the time and space in which to seize the initiative defensively was limited. From a Japanese perspective, the wrong initial choices unfortunately began to crowd out the possibilities that different decisions might have created at the beginning of a long conflict. It is important to recognize, however, that Japan's military defeat was not predetermined by her potentially unfavorable geopolitical position or the imbalance of latent military power between her and her enemies. Defeat came directly from how Japan managed and fought her war. Major military opportunities that could have been exploited were not.

To move to a more general assessment, beyond the specific means by which history might have been altered, our case also needs to estimate what the overall impact of such changes might have been. It should be clear by now that the Japanese had the capability to have fought a different and more successful war in the Pacific and that if they had done so the result would have been, at the least, a substantial delay in the establishment of the type of conditions that led to surrender in August 1945. The examples fleshed out in the various chapters of this book make a delay of the ending of the Pacific War of a year or more not at all an unreasonable possibility. But in that case, would the end of the war still have resembled its historical counterpart?

The standard argument against any exploration of a different ending to the war, and one that we encountered at the beginning of this book, is that the odds were so stacked against the Japanese that ultimately there was nothing they could have done to change the war's outcome. The material advantages of the Allies would have continued to grow. The defeat of Germany would have released even stronger Allied forces. The Americans would at some point have gotten close enough to unleash their strategic bombing campaign against the Home Islands. The Soviets would have invaded Manchuria. And, in any case, the atomic bomb, the secret ace in the hole, would have been ready for use in the late summer of 1945. Under the weight of such inevitabilities the Japanese would have had no choice but to surrender. Nothing essential in the historical endgame would have changed.

A slightly different argument is that even if the Japanese changed the way they fought in the Pacific, such changes would themselves have provoked alterations in the way the enemy fought its war. According to this view, the Allies historically proved themselves flexible and astute enough to have quickly come up with countermeasures to any changes in Japanese strategy or tactics that can be imagined. But this argument, of course, is itself a counterfactual reading of our counterfactual description of the war in the Pacific. It seems untenable to identify the most important factors that determined Japan's fate and at the same time insist that alterations in those factors would not have had the potential to produce important and different results. A year's delay in the Allied advance on Japan would have created a very different environment in which to play out the war's endgame.

What if Japan in mid-1945 was still far from defeat? Would the Soviets unilaterally have wanted to invade Manchuria in August 1945 if Japan's cities and factories were still untouched, her inner defenses largely intact, and the Americans still too far away or too bloodied to threaten the Home Islands directly? Soviet intervention was above all else opportunistic and dependent on prior American successes. The Soviets themselves possessed neither strategic air capability nor the amphibious forces to conquer Japan proper. We now know that the Japanese command was prepared to abandon Manchuria in order to bolster the forces gathering on Japan to resist the coming Allied invasion.[3] A Soviet agreement with Japan based on terms similar to those given to Finland in 1944 might have been a possibility. Extension of the war's end would also have given Allied suspicions of Soviet intentions and ambitions more time to ripen, lessening their desire for Russian interference, a process that was already well underway by the end of the war in Europe.

Events on the Asian mainland might also have outrun outcomes preferred by the Allies. As early as 1944, the Americans had lost interest in any direct military intervention on the Chinese coast. Given more incubation time, systematic Japanese depredations, widespread starvation, and a simmering civil war could have produced even more chaos in China. Fears of a more prolonged struggle leading to a Communist victory might have meant that it was more important for the Nationalists to reach an accommodation with Japan in exchange for the help of the millions of Japanese troops on the mainland to restore order. The Japanese were also the only force that could control the turmoil and political subversion that would have (and in some places already had) developed during a lengthened war in many former European colonies. The fate of Allied prisoners of war and the future of other groups facing yet another year under Japanese occupation would also have had to be factored in, on humanitarian grounds if nothing else.[4]

The abrupt and surprising end to the war caused by the atomic bombs has truncated our sense of alternate possibilities. Yet even the bombs' effectiveness was highly contextual: they were dropped after Japan had already come to the end of her rope. Under the different conditions that the extension of the war for another year might have produced, there may actually have been time to arrange a demonstration of the atomic bomb that would have convinced the responsible persons in the Japanese government that the war had to come to an end. American war weariness, the dreadful weight of the war's cost, and lack of sympathy for the reestablishment of European colonial rule in the East, may have led to a willingness to deal in a different manner with Japan to bring the war to an end. Growing public knowledge of the scale of Nazi atrocities may have helped temper the American view that the Japanese were somehow uniquely evil and inhumane. Some in the American military had already concluded by the spring of 1945 that an actual invasion of Japan would entail unacceptably high casualties. Rather than cling to its demand of unconditional surrender (which in any case did not finally apply to the emperor, the only authority capable of commanding the surrender of millions of troops) and risk the ignominy of destroying Japan by dropping one or two atomic bombs a month for the foreseeable future, the war-weary Allies might have been willing to accept a compromise peace that avoided the destruction and occupation of Japan proper but entailed the loss of her most recent conquests—a kind of *status quo ante*. The point here, however, is not to predict precisely the exact details of a different endgame and postwar, but rather to underline and appreciate the magnitudes of complexity that a more successful Japanese military resistance might have raised. As this book establishes, there was a real historical chance for Japan to have fought that better war.

NOTES

1. Dower, *War Without Mercy*, 15–32; quoted commentary on 17.
2. Overy, *Why the Allies Won*, 15.
3. Frank, *Downfall*, 221, 223.
4. These and indeed practically every important issue surrounding the war's ending are best treated in Frank, *Downfall*, passim. His study is the finest and, I believe, the final word on the final days of the Japanese empire.

Bibliography

Allen, Thomas B., and Norman Polmar. *Code-Name Downfall: The Secret Plan to Invade Japan—and Why Truman Dropped the Bomb*. New York: Simon & Schuster, 1995.

Appleman, Roy E., James M. Burns, et al. *Okinawa: The Last Battle. United States Army in World War II: The War in the Pacific*. Washington, DC: Office of the Chief of Military History, Department of the Army, 1948.

Arnold, Henry H. *The War Reports of . . . Marshall . . . Arnold . . . King. Reports of the Commanding General of the Army Air Forces on January 4, 1944, February 27, 1945, November 12, 1945*. Philadelphia, 1947.

Bath, Alan Harris. *Tracking the Axis Enemy: The Triumph of Anglo-American Naval Intelligence*. Lawrence: University Press of Kansas, 1998.

Bergerud, Eric M. *Touched With Fire: The Land War in the South Pacific*. New York: Viking Penguin, 1996.

———. *Fire in the Sky: The Air War in the South Pacific*. Boulder, CO: Westview Press, 2000.

Bix, Herbert P. *Hirohito and the Making of Modern Japan*. New York: Harper Collins, 2000.

Boyd, Carl, and Akihiko Yoshida. *The Japanese Submarine Force and World War II*. Annapolis, MD: Naval Institute Press, 1995.

Buruma, Ian. *The Wages of Guilt: Memories of War in Germany and Japan*. New York: Farrar Straus Giroux, 1994.

Butow, Robert J. C. *Japan's Decision to Surrender*. Palo Alto, CA: Stanford University Press, 1954.

Calvert, James F. *Silent Running: My Years on a World War II Attack Submarine*. New York: John Wiley & Sons, 1995.

Calvocoressi, Peter, Guy Wint, and John Pritchard. *Total War: The Causes and Courses of the Second World War*. vol. 2. *The Greater East Asia and Pacific Conflict*. New York: Pantheon Books, 1989.

Cameron, Craig M. *American Samurai: Myth, Imagination, and the Conduct of Battle in the First Marine Division, 1941–1951.* New York: Cambridge University Press, 1994.

Cannon, M. Hamlin. *Leyte: The Return to the Philippines. United States Army in World War II: The War in the Pacific.* Washington, DC: OCMH, Department of the Army, 1954.

Carr-Gregg, Charlotte. *Japanese Prisoners of War in Revolt: The Outbreaks at Featherston and Cowra during World War II.* New York: St. Martin's Press, 1978.

Cate, James L., and Wesley F. Craven. *The Army Air Forces in World War II: Men and Planes.* Chicago: University of Chicago Press, 1955.

Chang, Iris. *The Rape of Nanking: The Forgotten Holocaust of World War II.* New York: Basic Books, 1997.

Coakley, Robert W., and Richard M. Leighton. *Global Logistics and Strategy, 1940–1943.* Washington, DC: OCMH, Department of the Army, 1955.

———. *Global Logistics and Strategy, 1943–1945.* Washington, DC: OCMH, Department of the Army, 1968.

Condon-Rall, Mary Ellen, and Albert E. Cowdrey. *The Medical Department: Medical Service in the War Against Japan.* Washington, DC: Center of Military History, United States Army, 1998.

Connaughton, Richard. *The War of the Rising Sun and Tumbling Bear: A Military History of the Russo-Japanese War.* London: Routledge, 1991 (1998).

Connaughton, Richard, John Pimlott, and Duncan Anderson. *The Battle for Manila: The Most Devastating Untold Story of World War II.* Novato, CA: Presidio Press, 1995.

Coox, Alvin D. *Nomonhan: Japan Against Russia, 1939.* 2 vols. Palo Alto, CA: Stanford University Press, 1985.

———. "The Effectiveness of the Japanese Military Establishment in the Second World War." In Allan R. Millett and Williamson Murray, eds. *Military Effectiveness* 3:1–44. Boston: Allen & Unwin, 1988.

Cowdrey, Albert E. *Fighting for Life: American Military Medicine in World War II.* New York: The Free Press, 1994.

Cowley, Robert, and Steven Ambrose, eds. *What If? The World's Foremost Military Historians Imagine What Might Have Been.* New York: Putnam, 1998.

Craven, Wesley F., and James L. Cate. *The Pacific: Guadalcanal to Saipan, August 1942–July 1944.* vol. 4. Chicago: University of Chicago Press, 1950.

———. *The Pacific: Matterhorn to Nagasaki, June 1944 to August 1945.* vol. 5. Chicago: University of Chicago Press, 1953.

Crowl, Philip A. *The War in the Pacific: Campaign in the Marianas.* Washington, DC: OCMH, Department of the Army, 1960.

Crowl, Philip A., and Edmund G. Love. *The War in the Pacific: Seizure of the Gilberts and Marshalls.* Washington, DC: OCMH, Department of the Army, 1955.

Deutsch, Harold C., and Dennis E. Showalter, eds. *What If? Strategic Alternatives of World War II.* Emperor's Press, 1997.

Dower, John W. *War Without Mercy: Race and Power in the Pacific War.* New York: Pantheon, 1986.

———. *Japan in War and Peace: Selected Essays.* New York: New Press, 1993.

———. *Embracing Defeat: Japan in the Wake of World War II.* New York: W. W. Norton & Co., 1999.

Drea, Edward J. *MacArthur's Ultra: Codebreaking and the War Against Japan.* Lawrence: University Press of Kansas, 1992.
———. *In the Service of the Emperor: Essays on the Imperial Japanese Army.* Lincoln: University of Nebraska Press, 1998.
Dreyer, Edward L. *China at War, 1901–1949.* New York: Longman, 1995.
Dull, Paul S. *A Battle History of the Imperial Japanese Navy (1941–1945).* Annapolis, MD: United States Naval Institute Press, 1978.
Dunnigan, James F. *Victory at Sea: World War II in the Pacific.* New York: William Morrow and Company, 1995.
Dunnigan, James F., and Albert A. Nofi. *The Pacific War Encyclopedia.* New York: Checkmark Books, 1998.
Edgerton, Robert B. *Warriors of the Rising Sun: A History of the Japanese Military.* New York: W. W. Norton & Co., 1997.
Ellis, John. *Brute Force: Allied Strategy and Tactics in the Second World War.* New York: Viking Penguin, 1990.
———. *World War II: The Encyclopedia of Facts and Figures.* New York: Doubleday, 1993.
———. *World War II: The Encyclopedia of Facts and Figures.* USA: Military Book Club, 1993.
Fahey, James J. *Pacific War Diary, 1942–1945.* New York: Houghton Mifflin, 1991, reprint of 1963.
Feifer, George. *Tennozan: The Battle of Okinawa and the Atomic Bomb.* New York: Tickner & Fields, 1992.
Flanagan, General E. M., Jr. *Corregidor: The Rock Force Assault, 1945.* Novato, CA: Presidio Press, 1995.
Frank, Richard B. *Guadalcanal: The Definitive Account of the Landmark Battle.* New York: Random House, 1990.
———. *Downfall. The End of the Imperial Japanese Empire.* New York: Random House, 1999.
Friedman, Kenneth I. *Afternoon of the Rising Sun: The Battle of Leyte Gulf.* Novato, CA: Presidio Press, 2001.
Gilbert, Oscar E. *Marine Tank Battles in the Pacific.* Conshohocken, PA: Combined Publishing, 2001.
Gilmore, Allison B. *You Can't Fight Tanks with Bayonets: Psychological Warfare against the Japanese Army in the Southwest Pacific.* Lincoln: University of Nebraska Press, 1998.
Griffith, Thomas E. *MacArthur's Airman: General George C. Kenney and the War in the Southwest Pacific.* Lawrence: University Press of Kansas, 1998.
Hammel, Eric. *Guadalcanal: Decision At Sea. The Naval Battle of Guadalcanal, November 13–15, 1942.* Pacifica, CA: Pacifica Press, 1988.
Harries, Meirion, and Susie Harries. *Soldiers of the Sun: The Rise and Fall of the Imperial Japanese Army.* New York: Random House, 1991.
Hayashi, Saburo. *Kōgun: The Japanese Army in the Pacific War.* Quantico, VA: Marine Corps Association, 1989.
Hayes, Grace Person. *The History of the Joint Chiefs of Staff in World War II.* Annapolis, MD: Naval Institute Press, 1982.
Healy, Mark. *Midway, 1942: Turning Point in the Pacific.* Hong Kong: Osprey Publishing, 1996 (1993).

Honda, Katsuichi. *The Nanking Massacre*. Trans. Karen Sanders, ed. Frank Gibney. Armonk, NY: M. E. Sharpe, 1999.

Humphreys, Leonard A. *The Way of the Heavenly Sword: The Japanese Army in the 1920's*. Palo Alto, CA: Stanford University Press, 1995.

Iriye, Akira. *Power and Culture: The Japanese-American War, 1941–45*. Cambridge, MA: Harvard University Press, 1981.

Isely, Jeter A., and Philip A. Crowl. *The U.S. Marines and Amphibious War: Its Theory, and Its Practice in the Pacific*. Princeton: Princeton University Press, 1951.

Jentschura, Hansgeorg, Dieter Jung, and Peter Mickel. *Warships of the Imperial Japanese Navy, 1869–1945*. Trans. Antony Preston and J. D. Brown. Annapolis, MD: Naval Institute Press, 1986 (1970).

King, Ernest J. *The War Reports of . . . Marshall . . . Arnold . . . Fleet Admiral Ernest J. King, Commander in Chief, United States Fleet and Chief of Naval Operations*. Philadelphia: J. B. Lippincott & Co., 1944–45.

Lamont-Brown, Raymond. *Kempeitai: Japan's Dreaded Military Police*. Gloucestershire, UK: Sutton Publishing, 1998.

Levine, Alan J. *The Pacific War—Japan Versus the Allies*. Westport, CT: Praeger, 1995.

Linderman, Gerald F. *The World Within War: Americans' Combat Experience in World War II*. New York: The Free Press, 1997.

Linn, Brian M. *Guardians of Empire: The U.S. Army and the Pacific, 1902–1940*. Chapel Hill: University of North Carolina Press, 1997.

Louis, Allen. *Burma: The Longest War, 1941–45*. London: Phoenix Press, 2000 (1984).

Luvaas, Jay. "Buna. 19 November 1942–2 January, 1943: A Leavenworth Nightmare," in Charles E. Heller and William A. Stofft, eds., *America's First Battles, 1776–1965*. Lawrence: University of Kansas Press, 1986, 186–225.

MacArthur, General Douglas. *The Reports of General MacArthur*. vol. 1, pt. 1. *The Campaigns of MacArthur in the Pacific*. Washington, DC: Department of the Army, 1966 (1950).

———. *The Reports of General MacArthur*. vol. 1, pt. 2 and supplement. *MacArthur in Japan: The Occupation: Military Phase*. Washington, DC: Department of the Army, 1966 (1950).

———. *The Reports of General MacArthur*. vol. 2, Part 1 & 2. *Japanese Operations in the Southwest Pacific Area*. Washington, DC: Department of the Army, 1966 (1950).

MacKenzie, Simon P. "The Treatment of Prisoners of War in World War II." *Journal of Modern History* 66, No. 3, September 1994.

Manchester, William. *Goodbye Darkness: A Memoir of the Pacific War*. New York: Dell, 1982.

Marshall, George C. *Biennial Reports of the Chief of Staff of the United States Army to the Secretary of War. 1 July 1939–30 June 1945*. Washington, DC: Center of Military History, United States Army, 1996.

Matloff, Maurice, and Edwin M. Snell. *Strategic Planning for Coalition Warfare, 1941–42*. Washington, DC: OCMH, Department of the Army, 1953.

Matloff, Maurice. *The War Department: Strategic Planning for Coalition Warfare, 1943–1944*. Washington, DC: OCMH, Department of the Army, 1959.

Miller, John. *Guadalcanal: The First Offensive. United States Army in World War II: The War in the Pacific*. Washington, DC: OCMH, Department of the Army, 1949.

———. *Cartwheel: The Reduction of Rabaul. United States Army in World War II: The War in the Pacific.* Washington, DC: OCMH, Department of the Army, 1959.

Millet, Allan R., and Williamson Murray. *Military Effectiveness: World War II.* vol. 3. Boston: Allen & Unwin, 1988.

Milner, Samuel. *Victory in Papua. United States Army in World War II: The War in the Pacific.* Washington, DC: OCMH, Department of the Army, 1957.

Milton, Keith M. *Subs Against the Rising Sun.* Las Cruces, NM: Yucca Tree Press, 2000.

Moran, Jim, and Gordon L. Rottman. *Peleliu 1944: The Forgotten Corner of Hell.* Oxford, UK: Osprey Publishing, 2002.

Morison, Samuel Elliot. *History of United States Naval Operations in World War II.* vol. 4. *Coral Sea, Midway and Submarine Actions: May 1942–August 1942.* Boston: Little, Brown & Co., 1949.

———. *History of United States Naval Operations in World War II.* vol. 5. *The Struggle for Guadalcanal, August 1942–February 1943.* Boston: Little, Brown & Co., 1949.

———. *History of United States Naval Operations in World War II.* vol. 6. *Breaking the Bismarks Barrier, 22 July 1942–1 May 1944.* Boston: Little, Brown & Co., 1950.

———. *History of United States Naval Operations in World War II.* vol. 3. *The Rising Sun in the Pacific, 1931–April 1942.* Boston: Little, Brown & Co., 1951.

———. *History of United States Naval Operations in World War II.* vol. 7. *Aleutians, Gilberts and Marshalls, June 1942–April 1944.* Boston: Little, Brown & Co., 1951.

———. *History of United States Naval Operations in World War II.* vol. 8. *New Guinea and the Marianas, March 1944–August 1944.* Boston: Little, Brown & Co., 1953.

———. *History of United States Naval Operations in World War II.* vol. 12. *Leyte: June 1944–January 1945.* Boston: Little, Brown & Co., 1958.

———. *History of the United States Naval Operations in World War II,* vol. 14. *Victory in the Pacific, 1945.* Boston: Little, Brown & Co., 1959.

———. *History of United States Naval Operations in World War II.* vol. 13. *The Liberation of the Philippines: Luzon, Mindanao, the Visayas, 1944–1945.* Boston: Little, Brown & Co., 1959.

———. *History of United States Naval Operations in World War II.* vol. 15. *Supplement and General Index.* Boston: Little, Brown & Co., 1962.

———. *The Two-Ocean War: A Short History of the United States Navy in the Second World War.* Boston: Little, Brown & Co., 1963.

Morton, Louis. *The Fall of the Philippines. United States Army in World War II: The War in the Pacific.* Washington, DC: OCMH, Department of the Army, 1953.

———. *Strategy and Command: The First Two Years.* Washington, DC: OCMH, Department of the Army, 1962.

Navy History Division. *United States Submarine Losses, World War II.* Washington, DC: U.S. Government Printing Office, 5th Printing, 1963.

Newman, Robert P. "Ending the War With Japan: Paul Nitze's 'Early Surrender' Counterfactual." *Pacific Historical Review:* 167–94. 1995.

———. *Truman and the Hiroshima Cult.* East Lansing: Michigan State University Press, 1995.

Nobile, Philip, ed. *Judgement at the Smithsonian: The Bombing of Hiroshima and Nagasaki.* New York: Marlowe & Co., 1995.

O'Connell, Robert L. *Sacred Vessels: The Cult of the Battleship and the Rise of the U.S. Navy.* New York: Oxford University Press, 1993.

Okumiya, Masatake, and Jiro Horikoshi with Martin Caidin. *Zero.* New York: ibooks, 2002 (1956).

O'Neill, Richard. *Suicide Squads: The Men and Machines of World War II Special Operations.* Guilford, CT: Lyons Press, 1999.

Overy, Richard. *Why the Allies Won.* New York: W. W. Norton & Co., 1995.

Padfield, Peter. *War Beneath the Sea: Submarine Conflict During World War II.* New York: John Wiley & Sons, 1995.

Parillo, Mark P. *The Japanese Merchant Marine in World War II.* Annapolis, MD: Naval Institute Press, 1993.

Piccigallo, Philip R. *The Japanese on Trial: Allied War Crimes Operations in the East, 1945–1951.* Austin: University of Texas Press, 1979.

Prados, John. *Combined Fleet Decoded: The Secret History of American Intelligence and the Japanese Navy in World War II.* New York: Random House, 1995.

Pritchard, John R., and Sonia M. Zaide., eds. *The Tokyo War Crimes Trial: Index and Guide.* 5 vols. International Military Tribunal for the Far East. The Tokyo War Crimes Trial. New York: Garland, 1981.

Rees, David. *The Defeat of Japan.* New York: Praeger, 1997.

Reister, Frank A., ed. *Medical Statistics in World War II.* Washington, DC: Office of the Surgeon General. Department of the Army, 1975.

Ross, Bill D. *Iwo Jima: Legacy of Valor.* New York: Vintage Books, 1986.

Ross, Steven T. *American War Plans, 1941–1945: The Test of Battle.* Portland, OR: Frank Cass, 1997.

Rottman, Gordon L. *Okinawa 1945: The Last Battle.* Oxford, UK: Osprey Publishing, 2002.

———. *Saipan & Tinian 1944: Piercing the Japanese Empire.* Oxford, UK: Osprey Publishing, 2002.

———. *Japanese Pacific Island Defenses, 1941–45.* Oxford, UK: Osprey Publishing, 2003.

———. *Guam 1941 & 1944: Loss and Reconquest.* Oxford, UK: Osprey Publishing, 2004.

———. *The Marshall Islands 1944: Operation Flintlock, The Capture of Kwajalein and Eniwetok.* Oxford, UK: Osprey Publishing, 2004.

Saburo, Ienaga. *The Pacific War, 1931–1945: A Critical Perspective on Japan's Role in World War II.* New York: Pantheon Books, 1978 (1968).

Sakai, Saburo, with Martin Caidin and Fred Saito. *Samurai!* New York: ibooks, 2001 (1957).

Schaller, Michael. *Douglas MacArthur: The Far Eastern General.* New York: Oxford University Press, 1989.

Skates, John R. *The Invasion of Japan: Alternative to the Bomb.* Columbia: University of South Carolina Press, 1994.

Sledge, Eugene B. *With the Old Breed at Peleliu and Okinawa.* New York: Oxford University Press, 1990.

Smith, Robert R. *The Approach to the Philippines.* United States Army in World War II: The War in the Pacific. Washington, DC: OCMH, Department of the Army, 1953.

———. *Triumph in the Philippines.* United States Army in World War II: The War in the Pacific. Washington, DC: OCMH, Department of the Army, 1963.

Smurthwaite, David. *The Pacific War Atlas, 1941–1945.* London: Mirabel Books Ltd., 1995.

Spector, Ronald H. *Eagle Against the Sun: The American War With Japan.* New York: Vintage Books, 1985.

Taaffe, Stephen. *MacArthur's Jungle War: The 1944 New Guinea Campaign.* Lawrence: University Press of Kansas, 1998.

Tanaka, Yuki. *Hidden Horrors: Japanese War Crimes in World War II.* Boulder, CO: Westview Press, 1996.

Tsouras, Peter G. *Rising Sun Victorious: The Alternate History of How Japan Won the Pacific War.* Mechanicsburg, PA: Stackpole Books, 2001.

Ugaki, Matome. *Fading Victory: The Diary of Admiral Matome Ugaki, 1941–1945.* Trans. Masatake Chihaya. Pittsburgh: University of Pittsburgh Press, 1991.

United States War Department. *Handbook on Japanese Military Forces.* Baton Rouge: Louisiana State University Press, 1991 (Report of TM-E 30-480, 1 October 1944).

Van der Vat, Dan. *The Pacific Campaign: World War II. The U.S.-Japanese Naval War, 1941–1945.* New York: Simon & Schuster, 1991.

Warner, Denis, and Peggy Warner. *The Sacred Warriors: Japan's Suicide Legions.* New York: Van Nostrand Reinhold Company, 1982.

Watson, Mark S. *The War Department Chief of Staff: Prewar Plans and Preparations.* Washington, DC: Historical Division, Department of the Army, 1950.

Weinberg, Gerhard L. *A World at Arms: A Global History of World War II.* New York: Cambridge University Press, 1994.

Werrell, Kenneth P. *Blankets of Fire: U.S. Bombers over Japan During World War II.* Washington, DC: Smithsonian Institution Press, 1996.

West, Philip, Steven I. Levine, and Jackie Hiltz, eds., *America's Wars in Asia: A Cultural Approach to History and Memory.* Armonk, NY: M .E. Sharpe, 1998.

Whitman, John W. *Bataan: Our Last Ditch: The Bataan Campaign, 1942.* New York: Hippocrene Books, 1990.

Willmott, Hedley P. *The Second World War in the East.* London: Cassel, 1999.

———. *The War With Japan: The Period of Balance, May 1942–October 1943.* Wilmington, DE: S. R. Books, 2002.

Wright, Derrick. *Iwo Jima 1945: The Marines Raise the Flag on Mount Suribachi.* Oxford, UK: Osprey Publishing, 2001.

———. *Tarawa 1943: The Turning of the Tide.* Oxford, UK: Osprey Publishing, 2001.

Yahara, Hiromichi. *The Battle for Okinawa.* New York: John Wiley & Sons, 1995.

Yamamoto, Masahiro. *Nanking. Anatomy of an Atrocity.* Westport, CT: Praeger Publishers, 2000.

Young, Louise. *Japan's Total Empire: Manchuria and the Culture of Wartime Imperialism.* Berkeley: University of California Press, 1998.

Index

vs. military, 47; destruction, 49, 55;
losses, 45; organization, 55–56;
outcomes, 53; protection of, 40,
47–50, 56. *See also* convoys
Midway, 3–4, 16–19, 24, 27, 75–77,
93, 95, 122; possible outcomes in,
37; and submarines, 63
mines, 103
Molotov cocktails, 103
Moscow, 37

Nanking, 119
National Defense Zone, 14, 17, 19,
30–31, 38–41, 53, 113; Allies in, 43;
defense of, 114; effectiveness of, 40,
43–44; and submarines, 66
nationalism, 124; Chinese, 8
navies, importance of, 73–75
Navy General Staff (NGS), 12, 17, 62
Nazism, 125
Nelson, Horatio, 78
Netherlands. *See also* ABCD group
New Caledonia, 15–18
New Georgia, 97
New Guinea, 18–19, 27–28, 40, 75;
Allies in, 82–83; defense of, 43;
disease in, 43; opportunities of,
116; seizure of, 32; strategic
significance of, 109; troops in,
111
New Submarine Doctrine, 65
New Zealand, 18
Nimitz, Chester, 30, 74, 81, 108, 115
Nomonhon, 104–5

Okinawa, 31, 83, 88, 106, 108; defense
of, 113–14; kamikaze attacks in, 87,
96, 99; strategic significance of, 98;
U.S. losses in, 115
Onishi, Vice Admiral, 96
Operation Olympic, 81
Outer Perimeter, 17–19, 24, 31, 38
overextension, 16, 18, 38, 77, 79, 89,
122
Overy, Richard, 2, 120
Owen Stanley Mountains, 18, 27, 93
Ozawa, Jisaburo, 78, 82

Pacific Area forces, 18
Pacific Area of Operations, 43
Pacific Fleet, 12, 16, 43, 76;
amphibious capabilities, 108
Pacific War: endgame, 3, 41, 123, 124;
and Europe, 81; possible outcomes
of, 2–7, 24, 33, 37, 57, 79–80,
104–5, 119–23
Panama Canal, 61, 64
Parillo, Mark, 47, 57
Paulus, 42, 51
Pearl Harbor, 15–16, 30, 63; and air
war, 91; military opportunities in,
78; planning of, 12; as port, 64;
possible outcomes, 37; as submarine
base, 48, 62; and submarines, 59
Pelieu, 44, 106; defense of, 114
Penang, 64
petroleum, 9, 63
Philippines, 12, 14, 28; attacks on, 96;
battles of, 81–82; invasion of, 30;
Japanese defense in, 41; kamikaze
attacks in, 87; liberation of, 30; loss
of, 115; and merchant marine
routes, 51; strategic significance of,
98, 108; as strategic stronghold, 40;
strategies of, 32, 83; and
submarines, 60
planes. *See* airpower
Plan Orange, 106
Port Moresby, 14–15, 18, 27
Prados, John, 82
Prelude to War, 119
propaganda, 119
pro-war sentiment, American, 9
psychiatric casualties, 88

Quadrant Conference, 32

Rabaul, 12, 15, 18, 27–30, 51; as base,
93; counteroffensive of, 83; defense
of, 43; Japanese defense in, 42;
strategic significance of, 97
racism, 4
radar, 61–62, 84
Reports of General MacArthur, 45
risk theory, 73, 75–76, 78, 81, 84

About the Author

Professor James B. Wood of Williams College, a distinguished historian of early modern France, has been interested in military history since an early age. His most recent book, *The King's Army: Warfare, Soldiers, and Society During the Wars of Religion in France, 1562–1576,* received the Society for Military History's Distinguished Book Award in 1998. *Japanese Military Strategy in the Pacific War: Was Defeat Inevitable?* is his first print foray into modern military history. At Williams since 1973, he teaches courses on World War I, World War II, war in European history, the origins of modern warfare and generalship, and America's small wars. Despite his long-standing interest in warfare, he has never served in the military. He lives peacefully in Williamstown, Massachusetts, with his wife Margaret and the youngest of their three children as well as a young yellow Labrador.